MUSICAL NATIONALISM

Recent titles in
Contributions in American Studies
Series Editor: Robert H. Walker

Boosters and Businessmen: Popular Economic Thought and Urban Growth
in the Antebellum Middle West
Carl Abbott

Democratic Dictatorship: The Emergent Constitution of Control
Arthur Selwyn Miller

The Oriental Religions and American Thought:
Nineteenth-Century Explorations
Carl T. Jackson

Contemporaries:
Portraits in the Progressive Era by David Graham Phillips
Louis Filler, editor

Abortion, Politics, and the Courts:
Roe v. Wade and Its Aftermath
Eva R. Rubin

An Anxious Democracy: Aspects of the 1830s
John J. Duffy and H. Nicholas Muller, III

Artistic Voyagers: Europe and the American Imagination in the
Works of Irving, Allston, Cole, Cooper, and Hawthorne
Joy S. Kasson

Toward Increased Judicial Activism: The Political Role of
the Supreme Court
Arthur Selwyn Miller

Lawyers v. Educators: Black Colleges and Desegregation in
Public Higher Education
Jean L. Preer

The Nuyorican Experience: Literature of the
Puerto Rican Minority
Eugene V. Mohr

Business and Its Environment: Essays for Thomas C. Cochran
Harold Issadore Sharlin, editor

Sources for American Studies
Jefferson B. Kellogg and Robert H. Walker, editors

A New World Jerusalem: The Swedenborgian
Experience in Community Construction
Mary Ann Meyers

MUSICAL NATIONALISM

American Composers' Search for Identity

ALAN HOWARD LEVY

CONTRIBUTIONS IN AMERICAN STUDIES, NUMBER 66

GREENWOOD PRESS
WESTPORT, CONNECTICUT • LONDON, ENGLAND

ML
200.5
.L48
1983

9/85

Library of Congress Cataloging in Publication Data

Levy, Alan Howard.
    Musical nationalism.

    (Contributions in American studies, ISSN 0084-9227 ;
no. 66)
    Bibliography: p.
    Includes index.
    1. Music—United States—History and criticism.
2. Music—History and criticism—20th century.
3. Nationalism in music. I. Title. II. Series.
ML200.5.L48   1983   781.773   82-12168
ISBN 0-313-23709-3 (lib. bdg.)

Library of Congress Catalog Card Number: 82-12168
ISBN: 0-313-23709-3
ISSN: 0084-9227

First published in 1983

Greenwood Press
A division of Congressional Information Service, Inc.
88 Post Road West
Westport, Connecticut 06881

Printed in the United States of America

96602

10 9 8 7 6 5 4 3 2 1

CONTENTS

PREFACE

The art world of Paris in the twenties has been a rich source for the historian. What a brilliant array of people! But while much of this story has been told and retold, some important parts have been neglected, notably the activities of American composers. The neglect is doubtless due to the fact that the technical aspects of music are foreign to most historians. Indeed, music has generally, and unfortunately, been untouched by the cultural historian.

Several themes enter the story of American composers in Paris: the ways music did and did not fit into the general artistic activity of the Left Bank, the transmission of musical ideas from France to the United States and from the United States to France, the schooling Americans pursued in France, and the general interests of Americans in going to France. The last of these is the most complicated and inclusive. Like many who went to Paris, American musicians—Aaron Copland, George Antheil, Roy Harris, Roger Sessions, Virgil Thomson—disliked the stodgy old mores into which their country seemed to be relapsing after the Great War. Yet at the same time these Americans spoke of wanting to put America on the musical map, to see American music mature, and to come to grips with an American musical personality. This view, in contrast with the traditional expatriate disgust with America and the resulting anational or international approach to art, seems nationalistic. For American composers, nationalism and expatriation were not contradictory but complementary. The "old ways" of composing, the symphonic styles of Schumann and Brahms, rejection of which was symbolized by the exodus to France, opposed development of a national musical character. Conflict arose, then, between "national identity" and a "proper" course of action for a composer. The development of this conflict, as shown in American-French cultural exchange in postwar Paris, may be likened to the final act of a drama, both tragic and comic, centering on the quest of American musicians for exceptionalism.

In France in the twenties, many elements of American music came together that had theretofore been kept apart. Thus discussion must focus first on the developments that originally pulled apart art elements and vernacular elements and then on the gradual, almost tortuous, process of their unification through the French experiences of Copland, Thomson, and others. Developments in the art music world follow. Driven apart from each other, the art music world and the vernacular music world were two distinct spheres. (Various terms exist in musical nomenclature—classical/popular, cultivated/vernacular—none of which are totally satisfactory. I shall use the terms art and vernacular.) A focus on either music world is intellectually justifiable, as each has its own story. Neither the history of American art music nor that of American vernacular music from 1865 to 1930 has been fully told. Both need telling. Here I shall be dealing primarily with developments in the sphere of art music.

From 1865 to 1930 the often-frustrating efforts to integrate American art and vernacular musical elements were part of a broader search for cultural identity. These were years of maturation in virtually every facet of American society. Convinced of successful national growth in the economic, military, and scientific sectors, Americans held similar hopes for such fields of endeavor as the arts and music. But opinions varied as to how this could be done, ranging between two opposing positions. On the one hand, some looked exclusively to the nation's many racial, vernacular, ethnic, and regional traditions. Others advocated involvement in the cultural traditions of Europe. Many preferred some combination of the two, but the holders of the extreme positions were so tenacious as to forbid combination.

The choice of direction was a profound one; it held implications not only for music but for broader questions of national identity and political ideology. To those who took either extreme the course was straightforward. They either turned to folkways or to the latest developments in Europe, and they ignored, and often cast aspersions on, the other view. For those who preferred a combination of art and vernacular elements, the issue was complicated. Training in art music meant formal study, usually at a music conservatory in New York or Boston, or in Europe. The elitism at these locales vis à vis the American vernacular was strong and infectious. Consequently many American music students virtually were indoctrinated to consider their vernacular heritage as unworthy of attention. In this discussion I shall defend the "combining" approach. A national culture cannot exclude any good element within it, be it art or vernacular, without being elitist. Any elitism has to be overcome. After 1930 the confluence of musical styles in the United States and Europe began to blur lines denoting genres and revealed the elitisms required to maintain the vernacular/art music dichotomy. Indeed, in the art music world the elitism was never defeated through frontal attack; rather, this world itself went through a circuitous series of changes which resulted in the breakdown of the established tradition of distinguishing as separate genres the art music and vernacular elements in American music.

One of the principal causes of these developments was the shifting of international ties in American art music from 1865 to 1930. The chief shift was the decline of German influences and the rising importance of France in music education and compositional style. The Czech composer Antonín Dvořák was also important here and at times Russian music, particularly through Igor Stravinsky. Most important, however, was France, for it was there that Americans first encountered a tradition that did not reinforce the separation of art and vernacular music.

Two figures, despite their stature, will be largely absent from this discussion: Charles Ives and George Gershwin. This is the story of the interaction between music and certain cultural forces; Ives and Gershwin worked outside many of these. Changes in pedagogical methods and in the institutions where Americans studied are an important component of this story. Philosophies of music education dominant in the late nineteenth and early twentieth centuries supported the vernacular/art music dichotomy and were a part of the shifting international influences. The topic of education in the forces that shape a composer thus requires that little attention be paid to George Gershwin. He did indeed escape some of the art/vernacular divisions in his own writings, but he did so on his own. That such a genius did not fall into the dichotomy may be evidence for its basic poverty, and for the wisdom of "combining." Gershwin wanted to study with some important pedagogues, but each (Nadia Boulanger, Stravinsky, Maurice Ravel) refused him, feeling his talent was best left to develop on its own. Lacking his genius, however, other composers needed instruction in the fundaments of composition. Changes in the norms of Americans' music education are thus an important part of our discussion, while the career of George Gershwin is not.

Ever present in the late nineteenth century and early twentieth century were battles between composers and critics alarmed at the use of "vulgar" vernacular elements, technical innovations, particularly in harmony, or both. As with the developments in music education, this is no mere aside. For such dialogue did and does influence the directions composers pursue. Psychologically and financially, composers benefit from critical praise, from the popularity it may presage, even shape, and from performances of their music. As this attention was important among the forces upon American composers in the years in question, little attention will be given to Ives, despite the fact that he is sometimes considered a fundamentally American composer. Ives generally refrained from battles with tradition-bound critics, but he did so in a curious way. He often expressed contempt for various music institutions, schools, teachers, students, publishers, editors, and critics. Yet at the same time he wanted very much to be listened to, loved, and appreciated. On the one hand, then, to criticism that a given song could not be sung, he responded, "Don't sing it"—implying that the expression of ideas transcended any mere matter of performance or communication. On the other hand, he helped finance Nicholas Slonimsky's tour of Europe, where the latter performed some of Ives's music. Ives believed music and art should be attuned to everyday experience, yet a great many elements of his life were terribly aloof and isolated. This hate/love, all-or-nothing character of Ives renders him enigmatic for historians. But be one's judgment positive or negative, Ives's avoidance of the musical marketplace and lack of influence on other composers till the late thirties and forties renders his case an isolated one, not much entwined with or influencing of other events.

Gershwin's genius required little of the traditional pedagogical course and received little exposure to its shaping forces. Ives possessed sufficient financial resources to avoid the forces of exposure defiantly. Virtually none of the other American composers shared Gershwin's melodic gifts, or Ives's financial ones. The rigors of imposed study and the musical marketplace shaped them and the course of American musical history. To this story of musical, pedagogical, and social interaction and growth we now turn.

Risking hubris, I hope the quality of those to whom I am intellectually indebted reveals something of the content of the ensuing discussion. Daniel Rodgers of Princeton University, my major professor in graduate school, rendered every possible form of assistance regarding content and style. He is to me what Nadia Boulanger was to students of musical composition. Paul Conkin of Vanderbilt University, who always told me he was tone deaf, was ever relentless in his insistence on clarity of thought and expression. John Barker of the University of Wisconsin, with his record collection of, to date, 20,000 albums, was most generous with his wealth of information, always at his fingertips. To Robert Monschein and Walter Gray of the Wisconsin School of Music, I owe a special debt for much kind help. I owe much to Ednah Thomas, editor extraordinaire; as I once said to her: "Without your help this book would not have been written so good by me." Many thanks to my friends who patiently listened to my zany musings, and a special thanks to my dear friend Sylvia Kadushin, the most perceptive individual I know.

MUSICAL NATIONALISM

1 THE GERMAN ORTHODOXY

From the end of the American Civil War into the early twentieth century, Germany dominated the world of American art music. Early in their influence, German traditions aided American art music in such areas as compositional style and pedagogy. By 1910, however, these traditions had largely outlived their usefulness. Ossified though they were, German traditions fit snugly as an aesthetic counterpart to many sensibilities of early twentieth-century American social elites. Not until the Great War was this German connection severed.

Comparing the music of the leading American composer in 1865—Louis Moreau Gottschalk (1829-1869)—to that of major figures of the late nineteenth century—John Knowles Paine, George Chadwick, and Horatio Parker—reveals both the positive and the negative contributions of the Germans. Gottschalk wrote melodically pleasing and often virtuoso music, containing elements from a variety of cultures. Born in New Orleans's French Quarter, then a French-speaking enclave, and schooled in Paris, he had been exposed to many musics—Creole, French, Latin American, Caribbean, black American, West African, and southern American, as well as European art music. He used fragments of these many genres in various combinations in his work. In his compositions one finds exposition of ideas and repetition with varying instrumental color, but few such technical devices as contrapuntal development or smooth transitions between different melodic ideas. Gottschalk's music was like the writing of a promising but immature student, whose thoughts are interesting but who has yet to learn to explore nuances and enrich his ideas.

Other composers of the time, like George F. Bristow and William Fry, achieved a bit more technically and in doing so turned slightly away from the vernacular elements in Gottschalk. The drive for technical proficiency led later composers to seek the best music education. Between 1865 and 1890, with American music schools in their infancy, one had to go to Europe. Previously some Americans had studied in Europe, notably Lowell Mason. But the post-Civil War years marked the first time that Americans went abroad in large numbers, producing the first generation of American composers for whom European experiences shaped a collective stylistic identity.

It was natural for young artists to seek the most prestigious schools, to work with the greatest artists. For painters that meant going to Paris, for composers, Germany. With the wave of German immigrants to the United States after the Revolution of 1848, Americans witnessed a whole host of excellent German virtuosi, performance groups, and conductors. German music became a standard for American musical aspirations. Since the time of Haydn, Germany and Austria had dominated the world of art music. American composers from 1865 to 1900—Paine, Parker, Chadwick, William Mason, Arthur Weld, Arthur Whiting, Wilson Smith, Frank van der Stucken, Dudley Buck, Frederick Gleason—studied in Germany and wrote in styles similar to those of the German masters. The primary German tradition to which Americans tied themselves was that of Schumann and Brahms and their followers, who stood in opposition to many of the innovations of Berlioz, Liszt, and Wagner. While embracing the youthful, subjective, emotional modes of Romantic expression, Brahms and Schumann had felt that it should always take place within Classical forms. The new music of Liszt and Wagner they saw as having abandoned these forms or as toying too freely with their structural components. Such activity smacked of indulgence or spiritual decadence, while they themselves represented a combination of freedom and control, feeling and reason, and thus, in music, the expressions of the soul within Classical structures. Their prescription for students, including the Americans, was immersion in the Classical literature of Haydn, Mozart, Beethoven, and Schubert and acquisition of the structural details of Classical forms, so that emotions and feelings would find expression in something more concrete and enduring than mere personal fantasy.

This approach had both positive and negative effects on Americans. Gaining technical rigor was of paramount value, and composers like Paine, Parker and Chadwick were indeed more proficient at their craft than any Americans before them. Some of their works still continue to speak to a sensitive audience. Paine's Mass in D (1866), for example, still imparts the depth of tragedy and compassion Americans experienced during the Civil War. But some of their works communicated little more than pretty sounds and clear forms. For many American composers, unfortunately, the standards encountered in Germany became something for the mind to memorize, nor for the spirit to absorb. Chadwick, for example, in his *Symphonic Sketches* (1907), presented principal themes in the violas with the violins accompanying and embellishing in higher registers, a virtual mime of Brahms. Paine's *Spring Symphony* (1879) was similar in style and organization to Joachim Raff's work of the same name written a year earlier. His *Island Fantasy* showed his harmonic language to be heavily, perhaps overly, influenced by Mendelssohn. Even the Americans stylistically closer to Wagner—Dudley Buck and Frederick Gleason— were most un-Wagnerian in their rather pedestrian renditions of leitmotif. Indeed, Wagner had no true descendant. His close followers, like Buck and Gleason, and even such a talent as Humperdink, carved but small niches in music annals. Other descendants, like Mahler, Strauss, Debussy, and Schoenberg, who not only drew from Wagner but from non-Wagnerian, Classical traditions as well, achieved much more; this reveals some of the wisdom in Brahms's critique of the "new music" as unable to sustain itself or avoid perversion in future generations. The limitations of post-Wagnerians also indicate the good fortune in America's tie to Schumann and Brahms, considering the nation's drive for a lasting national tradition.

Nineteenth-century American miming of European masters prompted Aaron Copland to comment on his predecessors: "A genteel aura hangs about them; no one expired in the gutter like Edgar Allan Poe. [They] were in their instincts overgentlemanly, too well-mannered, and . . . reflected a certain museumlike propriety and bourgeois solidity."[1] As a leader of the generation that emerged in Paris in the 1920s, Copland was predisposed to see his German "ancestors" as stuffy and genteel. In conscious flight from many of their technical, pedagogical, and esthetic standards, Copland naturally painted a stark contrast. Indeed, some of the "German" generation's music appears stiff and mannered. Other works, Chadwick's operas *The Padrone* and *Tobasco*, for example, have a delightful earthiness. Parker's *Hora Novissima* is an oratorio of terrific passion. More importantly, Chadwick, Parker, and Paine were simply damn good composers, irrespective of style. Their absence from the twentieth-century concert stage reflects extramusical prejudices over which a late-nineteenth-century composer could not possibly have exerted any control. Paine, Parker, et al. were indeed members of the social elite and for this seem "overgentlemanly." Given their time and station they had little choice. The hard lines of social distinction were insurmountable for any mere composer who did not wish to commit professional suicide.

The sensibilities of certain American social elites reinforced many of the esthetic precepts of the German-trained Americans. Copland's adjectives "museumlike" and "bourgeois" were well chosen, considering the audiences and patrons for whom Paine, Parker, Chadwick, and others wrote. The tastes of established critics revealed that in the major music centers of the United States—New York and Boston—the Schumann-Brahms tradition reigned supreme. For example, John Sullivan Dwight, whose *Journal of Music* held sway in Boston and elsewhere from 1859 to 1881, denounced Wagner as representing "the very extreme of modern extravagance and willfulness in the spasmodic strife to be original."[2] Like many antebellum radicals, Dwight, a former Unitarian minister, Brook Farm participant, and abolitionist, appeared increasingly old-fashioned in the rapidly changing world that was America in the 1870s and 1880s. With horror he viewed the many changes he witnessed. He saw such groups as unionists and suffragists rising, full of conviction, bereft of a sense of historical roots. He witnessed the rapid urbanization of the American east coast and interior and all the accompanying problems of social and intellectual dislocation. The mass influx of immigrants seemed to him, by its sheer size and disorder and intensity, to be tearing at the fabric of society. Such changes paralleled, in his mind, many distasteful innovations in musical composition. In a letter to Georg Henschel, conductor of the Boston Symphony Orchestra (and a friend of Brahms), Dwight wrote, for example, of

> the *depressing* influence so much of the more ambitious music had upon my mind,—so many big words which, by their enormous orchestration, crowded harmonies, sheer intensity of sound, and restless, swarming motion without progress, seem to seek to carry the listeners by storm, by a roaring whirlwind of sound, instead of going to the heart of the simpler and divine way of "the still, small voice. . . . " When I meet a "red-hot" Wagnerite [or a champion of any modern composer], I am sometimes tempted in a humorous way to say the worst I can upon the other side.[3]

The tone of foreboding is significant here. Dwight saw Wagner as a musical radical who challenged established musical sensibilities in the same manner political radicals (like Wagner's friend Michael Bakunin) attacked broader social mores. Wagner's music, like Bakunin's politics, might be the wave of the future, but it was a wave moving so furiously that disaster was inevitable. Like Schumann, Dwight knew the writings of the late eighteenth- and early nineteenth-century German writers and philosophers—Goethe, Fichte, Schiller, Schopenhauer—and believed in the spiritual necessity of expressions of emotion and subjectivity. But like Schumann also, he felt this should take place within Classical models. Both equally distrusted any such expressions which lacked sufficient structural anchoring.

Other American music critics also distrusted "the music of the future." Wagner, wrote the *Cincinnati Commercial* in 1880, "may be the music of the future, but it will be heard in the realms of Pluto."[4] Imagery of the devil was quite common among critics of the modern music of the late nineteenth century. Regarding a symphony by Wagner's compatriot Franz Liszt, the *New York Sun* conjectured: "It seemed as though Beelzebub . . . stood at the composer's right hand while he scored this work."[5] Puckishly, the

Sun asked why Liszt did not "compose for each class of instruments in a different key."[6] The *Boston Gazette* similarly suggested that Liszt would be consistent with his aesthetic precepts if he instructed the members of the orchestra to play anything they wished, thus creating musical anarchy.[7] To these critics such compositions seemed forebodingly anarchical, and within forty years Charles Ives would be executing them. Critics compared "the future" with their older idols. Thus Liszt "was like playing one of Beethoven's symphonies backwards," and "placed on a program after Schumann," he was like "a wild boar in a drawing room."[8] Later, against innovators like Arnold Schoenberg, the venom continued. Henry T. Finck, a leading New York critic in the early twentieth century, wrote of Schoenberg: "He learned a lesson from militant suffragettes. He was ignored till he began to smash parlor furniture, throw bombs, and hitch together ten pianolas, all playing different tunes, whereupon everybody began to talk about him."[9] Finck believed an avant-gardist like Schoenberg simply must be trying to attract attention like a child. Like Dwight before him, Finck viewed as immature any art which seemed a mere personal outburst. He held to a conception of beauty which uplifted the spirit and stimulated the intellect through a creative exposition of ideas within a rational framework.

That these critics linked the music of the future with "suffragettes" or anarchy was significant, for they were men writing for audiences of symphony orchestras and operas, the social elite. Such metaphors as "a wild boar in a drawing room" presented easily recognizable images to these elites, not beleaguered by anarchists, populists, suffragists, and unionists who challenged many of the fundamentals of the social and economic order. In the refuge of the concert hall, the elitists did not enjoy similar attacks on their esthetic sensibilities.[10]

Because social and economic elites controlled the purse strings of the nation's artistic institutions, they could fend off such attacks. For composers who wanted their works performed and praised, the choice was clear: cater to audiences and earn rewards, or experiment and risk neglect. Many chose the former. The orthodoxy of Schumann and Brahms thus remained powerful for many years.

Aspects of postsecondary music education also contributed to the German domination of late nineteenth-century American art music. Few music conservatories existed in the United States before 1865, but over 100 had been established by 1900. In most cases the "bourgeois solidity" of the composers and critics permeated educational philosophy. Like the composers, the nation's best pedagogues were German trained. Fenelon Rice, for example, director of the Oberlin Conservatory of Music from 1869 to 1901, studied at the Leipzig Conservatory; when he took over at Oberlin he instituted the same sturcture that existed at his alma mater, the same theory requirements, the same "class method" as opposed to private instruction, even the same harmony texts.[11] As in Germany, little formal interaction took place between music schools and colleges and universities. In Germany informal relations existed, but in the United States most music schools were isolated, thus minimizing the innovations that could come through cross-disciplinary communication and entrenching of the pedagogical orthodoxy of American music. The nation's German-trained composers headed the major music schools. Chadwick was director of the New England Conservatory of Music in Boston from 1897 to 1931; Paine headed the music department at Harvard from 1867 to 1904; Parker ran the Yale School of Music from 1895 to 1918.

Paine's and Parker's relations with their respective parent institutions, while helping to link music with other fields, in other ways promoted further isolation and solidity. In both schools the idea of music in the curriculum was not altogether acceptable. Harvard historian Francis Parkman, for example, recalling Cato the Elder's incessant reminder to the Romans of the menace of Carthage, always ended meetings of the Harvard Corporation with "*musica delenda est*" (music must be destroyed). Further, he often prescribed the abolition of the music department when financial difficulties arose.[12] Despite Parkman, music gained a place at Harvard through the efforts of President Charles W. Eliot. During his long tenure, 1869 to 1909, Eliot restructured Harvard from a liberal arts college into a multifaceted university. Music, along with other fields like architecture, engineering, law, and medicine, fitted into the expanded curriculum he envisaged. The music department had to limit its pedagogy to respectable fields, in part to placate disgruntled traditionalists like Parkman. This meant dealing solely with speculative music—theory, history, and composition—and avoiding practical music—the study of instruments and voice. In traditional educational philosophy, as far back as Plato, *musica speculativa* was a legitimate intellectual pursuit, while *musica practica* was not. Accordingly, Paine kept Harvard's music curriculum strictly speculative. The Yale School of Music taught practical as well as speculative music, and it is more than coincidental that it did not gain full recognition from Yale College until 1945. Though it was part of the university, the college kept at arm's length the School of Music and other subjects outside the traditional nineteenth-century curriculum, such as art, architecture, engineering, medicine, and law.

Paine and Parker both strove hard to demonstrate the academic legitimacy of their fields. Parker, personally and professionally, created for the school and himself a social standing generally denied musicians at the time. People who knew him intimately said his dignified, aloof character extended from a fear, since he was a musician, of being taken for a bohemian.[13] David Stanley Smith, his successor at Yale, said Parker personified a "modernized Puritanism."[14] Parker's daughter noted that his impeccable manner of speech made strangers think him an Englishman.[15] An integral part of this manner was his conservative, thoroughly proper musical sensibility. He was a bright man, recalled Charles Ives, who was a pupil of Parker, "but content to remain tied to what Rheinberger [Parker's teacher at Munich] taught him."[16] Parker's compositional style stemmed from Brahms. He had little affection for such "decadents" as Wagner and even less for the major figures who followed, such as Debussy. Students with modernistic tendencies like Ives were thoroughly put off and had to knuckle under when attending Parker's classes in free composition. In addition to composition, Parker taught all music history classes at Yale, where he strongly emphasized the German traditions to which he was so tied. His text was Waldo Pratt's *History of Music*,[17] a book published in 1907 which remained unrevised in all the years Parker employed it. The chapters dealing with music since 1750, except for sections on French and Italian opera, are a history of Austro-German music with little treatment of any moderns. At Harvard, Paine was personally more fatherly than the austere Parker but no less proper in manner and traditional in compositional style. As a teacher of theory and history, he too emphasized Austro-German traditions almost exclusively.

Complementing the proper, conservative character of musicians like Parker and Paine and the schools they ran were their attitudes toward so-called popular music. "There are humbler levels of popular taste which are surely significant," wrote Parker.

> It is indeed stirring to hear a great mass of people, including a seven foot policemen, singing. . . . The policeman's eyes and attitude show sincerity and devotion. . . . He is moved by his vocal efforts and enjoys his emotion and singing. So do I, but I wish the music were such as I could swallow without gagging.[18]

At neither Harvard nor Yale was treatment given to any vernacular music. It was difficult enough to justify teaching the so-called higher genres of music at a university; teaching vernacular traditions would have been utterly unacceptable. Parker, for one saw no musicality in these "lower" genres anyway. As one of the major directions of music, and other arts in the twentieth century, was toward a breakdown of the high art-low art dichotomy, commitment by music educators to an unashamedly elitist outlook served to underscore the conservatism of American musical traditions.

In the music of Paine, Parker, or contemporaries like Chadwick, there is little evidence of vernacular music. Chadwick used vernacular traces in his Symphonic Sketches; in his opera *The Padrone*, with its remarkably earthy operatic theme of the hardships of Italian immigrants; and in two light operas *The Quiet Lodging* and *Tobasco*. Parker wrote a piece for the opening of John Wanamaker's department store in Philadelphia and included military bands and bugle corps. For concert works he was more proper. His opera *Mona*, based on native American material, was his major brush with the vernacular in any concert work. His free use of vernacular idioms at an outdoor celebration like the Wanamaker opening indicates the split in Parker's mind between music for the concert hall and that appropriate for "the mass, including a seven foot policeman." Within the concert hall this generation composed programmatic works either religious, like Parker's *Hora Novissima*, or of anationalistic bent, for example, Paine's *Spring* Symphony. Programs with historical or geographical focus, like Chadwick's *Tam O'Shanter*, were often not American based. Scottish traditions were legitimate sources of inspiration, but American materials, which Gottschalk had used so freely, smacked of the social genres which the nation's social and musical elite had transcended.

After Gottschalk the concern for technical proficiency led American composers into certain German traditions. As these traditions developed and took root in America, compositional and pedagogical norms emerged which the sensibilities and money of the nation's social leadership reinforced. The elite of American music became a reflection of the tastes of the social elite at large. But just as there were challenges to that broader socioeconomic leadership in the late nineteenth and early twentieth century, so too did grumblings from the music world emerge and seriously alter American music between 1890 and 1920.

NOTES

1. Aaron Copland, *Music and Imagination*, Charles Eliot Norton Lectures, Harvard University 1951-1952 (New York: Mentor, 1952), p. 108.

2. John Sullivan Dwight, *Dwight's Journal of Music*, January 9, 1875, p. 8.

3. Quoted in George Willis Cooke, *John Sullivan Dwight: Brook Farmer, Educator, Critic of Music* (Hartford: Transcendental Books, 1973), p. 67.

4. *Cincinnati Commercial*, May 18, 1880, p. 6.

5. *New York Sun*, April 4, 1870, p. 11.

6. Ibid.

7. *Boston Gazette*, November 22, 1880, p. 10.

8. Ibid., and *New York Sun*, April 4, 1870, p. 11.

9. Henry T. Finck, *Musical Progress* (New York: Harper and Brothers, 1923). p. 78.

10. Such a theory smacks of "status anxiety," a greatly overused theory which historians have tried to apply to many controversial social groups. Perhaps the most probing analysis of this theory is that of Robert Berkhofer, who wrote that the status anxiety theory works only if the particular person or group in question looks exclusively to the past and suggests no new course of action (*A Behavioral Approach to Historical Analysis* [New York: Free Press, 1969], pp. 70-72). This effectively negates well-known applications of the theory to populists, to progressives, or to other reformers of the late nineteenth and early twentieth century. But among the music critics, and the elites they represented, who apotheosized Beethoven, Schumann, and Brahms, the theory fits better.

11. R. D. Skyrum, "Oberlin Conservatory, A Century of Musical

Growth" (Ph.D. dissertation, University of Southern California, 1963), pp. 76-77, 97.

12. Quoted in Gilbert Chase, *America's Music*, 2d rev. ed. (New York: McGraw-Hill Book Co., 1966), p. 336.

13. Frank R. Rosseter, *Charles Ives and His America* (New York: Liveright, 1975), p. 60.

14. David Stanley Smith, "A Study of Horatio Parker," *Musical Quarterly* 16 (April 1930), p. 157.

15. Isabel Parker Semler, *Horatio Parker: A Memoir for His Grandchildren Compiled from Letters and Papers* (New York: G. P. Putnam's Sons, 1942), p. 94.

16. Quoted in Henry Cowell and Sidney Cowell, *Charles Ives and His Music* (New York: Oxford University Press, 1955), pp. 33-34.

17. Yale School of Music catalogs, 1917-1918, p. 14; 1918-1919, p. 11.

18. Horatio Parker, "Our Taste in Music," *Yale Review* 7 (July 1918), p. 782.

AMERICANISM AND FRENCH
2 IMPRESSIONISM

In the 1890s new styles of composition arose in Western music, notably French impressionism, and new approaches to composition, such as the use of vernacular materials. Both vernacularism and French impressionism marked departures from the academic, Germanic styles of Paine, Parker, and Chadwick. These new approaches and styles were often mutually exclusive, as vernacularists stridently opposed any links with musical genres that appeared elitist and impresssionists held to a high art-low art dichotomy. Their final combination in the writings of American composers after World War I at last drew American music away from nineteenth-century norms and began an integrated American musical personality.

Edward MacDowell (1861-1908), who flourished with the generation of Paine and Parker, presaged tendencies toward the French and slightly toward the vernacular (or at least away from the antivernacular). MacDowell violated the custom of the time by studying first in Paris (1876 to 1879), then in Germany (1878 to 1881). He spent his Paris years at the Conservatoire, where, along with his classmate Claude Debussy, he showed reluctance to follow prescribed patterns of composition. MacDowell had begun to go his own way, especially in harmony, with experiments in seventh and ninth chords. Leaving France for Frankfort, MacDowell studied piano under Carl Heymann and composition with Joachim Raff, two of the most open-minded German music professors of the time. Raff, a composer of considerable reputation, was interested in the harmonic experiments of Liszt and Wagner.

Though not as avant-garde as they, he was generally sympathetic toward innovation and encouraged MacDowell to try it. It was under Raff that MacDowell wrote one of his best early works, the Piano Concerto in A minor, op. 15 (1881). Raff approved it; Liszt liked it too. A striking characteristic of the work is its similarity to the piano concerto in the same key by the Norwegian composer Edvard Grieg. The opening of the third movement of the MacDowell concerto, a tremolo followed by a B diminished seventh chord, is a virtual copy of the beginning of Grieg's famous work, and the harmonic language and the interplay of dynamics between the piano and orchestra are also similar in both. Mac-Dowell later became a friend of Grieg. He may have felt an affinity for Grieg as another composer in similar artistic circumstances, trying to learn technique without becoming too German.

Carl Heymann also appreciated MacDowell's imagination and taught him new and refreshingly different ways of playing the established classics, particularly in allowing more freedom with regard to tempi. But this playing outraged more traditional pedagogues at Frankfort, notably Clara Schumann, and as a result when Heymann retired in 1881 and recommended MacDowell as his replacement, a move that Raff seconded, the rest of the faculty vetoed the proposal. MacDowell was only twenty, a factor no doubt considered, but Heymann's social unpopularity as an Orthodox Jew was also important. Thus in his European study MacDowell slapped tradition in the face; not only did he study in Paris, but also his two German masters worked outside conservative aesthetic norms, and in Heymann's case social norms as well.

MacDowell remained in Europe until 1888, when he returned to the United States and continued to compose. From this point MacDowell did not depart radically from the style he had learned in Europe. Though he continued to experiment harmonically, technically he was no more progressive than such Germans as Liszt and Wagner. Similarly, in his tone poetry he was no less, though no more, tied to the employed texts than they. All used a text as a take-off point for musical embellishment. But MacDowell's link with Liszt and Wagner placed him in a more progressive position than that of Paine, Chadwick, or Parker. Eventually his tonal language deviated much less from established methods than did Debussy's or even that of less progressive French composers such as Chausson, Lalo, or Fauré. Nonetheless he represents the beginnings of America's break with the compositional norms of Schumann and Brahms.

Later American composers expressed admiration for MacDowell because of his technical strengths, his willingness to experiment, and even more, his occasional use of "American" materials in his tone poetry: *New England Idyls, Indian Suite,* and *Woodland Sketches.* Sometimes he titled movements in English rather than in the traditional Italian, which also appealed to later nationalists. But just as his tonal language only hinted at future developments, MacDowell's "Americanism" had strict limits. He used American materials simply because they had musical value to him. American scenery was as useful to him as anything European, neither more nor less. Later vernacularists were to be strident in compensating for the old European domination, jingoistically posturing the worth of America, not as merely equal to Europe, but as superior. The "woodlands" of MacDowell's *Woodland Sketches* happened to be in New Hampshire, but he was merely asserting the beauty of the woods. He felt no need to tout New Hampshire; to do so would limit the appeal of a piece which MacDowell felt should move a German as much as a New Englander. "National music," he wrote, "has no place in art for its characteristics may be duplicated by anyone who takes the fancy to do so. On the other hand, the vital element in music—personality—stands alone. . . . Music that can be made by 'recipe' is not music, but 'tailoring.' "[1]

MacDowell did not advocate musical nationalism, a conscious illustration of the musical worth of a culture through the use of its vernacular elements, with an avoidance of any identifiably foreign musical elements. Nor did he radically depart from the technical norms of his time. He did provide inklings of future developments, setting the example of an imaginative composer who was simultaneously technically competent and forward looking in both subject matter and style. This example was important for future composers who wished to be technically proficient, identifiably American, and *à la page* with the avant-garde. "His music," wrote Aaron Copland, "shows more independence of spirit, and certainly more personality, than was true of his colleagues around 1900 [Paine, Parker, and Chadwick]. It was the music of MacDowell, among Americans, that we knew best, even in 1925."[2]

Under President Nicholas Murray Butler, MacDowell established a music department at Columbia University. The conflicts between the two men showed another contrast between MacDowell and his more orthodox contemporaries. Like Eliot at Harvard, Butler greatly expanded Columbia's curriculum in the late nineteenth century, but while he accepted music he wanted to keep it a discreet distance from Columbia College by making it part of the Teachers' College. MacDowell opposed this view, nor in general did he feel it necessary to adopt the stilted postures of his colleagues at Harvard and Yale. Conflicts with Butler prompted MacDowell's resignation in 1904 and contributed greatly to the nervous and physical exhaustion which brought on his mental collapse and, in 1908, premature death at forty-seven.

The unity of technical innovativeness and Americanism in MacDowell's music, and his forthrightness in pedagogy, would be largely absent for a generation after his death. Until the time of Copland, American composers were either nationalistic in content and old-fashioned in style or stylistically modern and anationalistic in content. Not until Copland and his generation emerged from Paris in the 1920s did modernism, Americanism, and technical proficiency unite.

In the 1890s, as part of the general nationalistic tenor of the time, came the first full wave of "Americanism" in art music. A prime force behind this development was the Czech composer Antonín Dvořák. Dvořák arrived in New York in October 1892 to become director of the National Conservatory of Music. During his tenure, 1892 to 1896, he studied the compositions of Gottschalk and Stephen Foster and black and native American folk music. Subsequently he wrote an arrangement of Foster's "Old Folks at Home" and revealed his study of native American and black idioms with the various devices—syncopation, scales lacking in fourths, sevenths, or leading tones, a minor scale with fourth, minor seventh, and no sixth, and pentatonic scales—in his Quartet, op. 96, *The American;* Quintet, op. 97, and in his better known Symphony in E Minor, op. 95, *From the New World.*

Dvořák not only steeped himself in American idioms but allowed his composition students to do the same. He also took on many new black students, procuring them scholarships if needed, and hired several black teachers.[3] Several of his pupils took the path of musical nationalism. Henry T. Burleigh and William Arms Fisher transcribed numerous black spirituals, Burleigh's "Deep River" being the most famous. Harvey Worthington Loomis became a prominent authority on Native American music and wrote several pieces, such as *Lyrics of the Red Man,* based on Native American materials. Rubin Goldmark, who later taught Aaron Copland and George Gershwin, developed an interest in both Native American and black music in works like *Hiawatha* and *Negro Rhapsody.*

American audiences were interested in their own musical heritage. Dvořák's arrival, on the four-hundredth anniversary of Columbus Day, was fortuitous. At Dvořák's first New York concert, Major Thomas W. Higginson, a prominent music patron of the day, spoke of "two worlds—the world of Columbus and the new world of music."[4] Columbus had discovered America geographically: Dvořák would help do so musically. "The Americans expect great things from me," Dvořák wrote to a friend in Prague. "The main thing is . . . to show them to the promised land and kingdom of a new and independent art, in short, to create a national music."[5] The reception of the premieres of Dvořák's Quartet, Quintet, and *New World* Symphony was enthusiastic. After the second performance of the *New World* Symphony, the *New York Herald* reported: "Even after he [Dvořák] had left his box and was walking about in the corridor the applause continued. And finally he returned to the gallery railing, and then what a reception he received! The musicians . . . applauded until the place rang again."[6] The *New York Tribune* told of a "loud, long, and enthusiastic" reaction to the Quartet and Quintet and went on to say that composers who wish to work in American folk material have in these two works "the clearest model before them."[7]

Yet it was not all smooth sailing with Dvořák's interest in native American and black music. On January 23, 1894, Dvořák presented a concert in New York emphasizing aspects of black music. It was the premiere for his arrangement of "Old Folks at Home," which he dedicated to Henry T. Burleigh, one of his black students, and Burleigh sang the bass solo supported by an all-black chorus. In an interview with the *New York Herald* Dvořák declared: "Negro melody furnishes the only sure base for an American school of music."[8] Audiences were indeed interested in the development of an American music, but they began to wonder if this music was to be based on the music of blacks and native Americans. For many middle-class white Americans such a thought was disquieting. Dvořák was either unaware of this sentiment or determined to counter it. Reviewing Dvořák's all-black concert, the *New York Herald* complimented Dvořák and Jeanette Thurber, benefactor of the conservatory, on their "noble deed" and remarked condescendingly how each singer "marked time with his head," implying that the concert would have been of greater interest to an anthropologist than to a musician.[9] When a composer of world stature like Dvořák employed black idioms in his own writings, critics could not be so flippantly patronizing. They then attempted to play down the influences on Dvořák's American motifs. Philip Hale, music critic of the *Boston Journal,* snorted: "The themes [of the *Quartet*] are characteristic—but not necessarily or inevitably characteristic of Negro temperament which seems now . . . to be regarded as synonymous with American temperament,"[10] and later wrote: "Negro airs . . . tint slightly two or three passages of the *New World Symphony* without injuring its Czech character."[11] Henry T. Finck, no friend of innovation, wrote of the *New World* Symphony's largo movement: "Nothing could be more ridiculous than the attempts that have been made to find anything black or red in the glorious soulful melody which opens the movement. . . . Nothing could be more white. . . . Only a genius could have written it."[12] Of the composer Henry T. Burleigh, Finck declared that "in his excellent songs [Burleigh was] more white than black."[13]

In spite of such hostility, many American composers pursued musical "Americanism" in the early twentieth century. Dvořák's students Henry Walley, Henry Rowe Shelley, and Will Marian Cook, like Burleigh, Fisher, Loomis, and Goldmark, continued in the steps of their master. Other Americans similarly inclined were Arthur Shepherd, Emerson Whithorne, Charles Cadman, Natalie Burlin, John Powell, Frederick Johnson, Harvey Gaul, and James Dunn, all drawing upon black, ethnic or native American motifs and finding inspiration in American locales or American literature.

Perhaps the most famous musical nationalists of the early twentieth century were Henry Gilbert, a pupil of MacDowell, and Arthur Farwell. Disgusted with the elitism of reactions to the use of so-called lower genres, Gilbert and Farwell were enthusiastic students of the music of native Americans and of former slaves, notating much of it for the first time and using some of the materials in their own compositions. As a result of the disdain for "lower" genres among critics and other elite music consumers, many "Americanists" were unable to get their music published. Accordingly, in 1901 Gilbert and Farwell founded the Wa-Wan Press, which published music by Americans without regard to genre— "Americanist" art music, popular music, and anationalistic art music as well. Gilbert and Farwell, in their reaction to one elitism, did not swing to the other extreme and fall into an antielitism of their own. Contemporary critics might well take note.

Not all American composers were turning to American vernacular traditions; others continued to look to Europe, but while critics and audiences were still listening to Brahms, younger Americans looked elsewhere. In 1900 the modern style in Western music was the impressionism of Claude Debussy and Maurice Ravel. In reaction to the excessive sentimentality and introspection of the Romantics, Impressionists developed a new style. Impressionist painters sought to create more than a mere reproduction of an object, now that the camera could do that. Rather, they focused on the emotions an image stirred. In the belief that the suggestion of an idea can be more powerful than the image in all its detail, painters sought merely to suggest an object. Musicians like Debussy worked in the same way. Rather than painting a musical picture with no nuance left to the imagination, they encouraged subjective impressions in the listener. To achieve this, painters turned away from extreme clarity of line, shortened their brush strokes, and developed more subtle gradations of color. Similarly, musicians wrote with intentional ambiguity in tonality and developed nuances of sound through odd chord combinations bordering on polytonality and atonality. As they wished to stimulate subjective impressions of a given object, composers wrote intervals, as painters created line, with intentional lack of clarity. They presented fourth, fifth and octave chords without filling in the mediant, for example, an octave chord in C—C-E-G-C—without the E. Along with such technical innovations, composers developed interests in other musics, those of Africa, Asia, and Medieval Europe, where they found examples for some of their experiments. Excited by these new techniques, some American composers in the early twentieth century began writing in this style: John Alden

Carpenter, Charles Thomlinson Griffes, Edward Burlingame Hill, Charles Martin Loeffler, Emerson Whithorne, Louis Gruenberg, Amy Beach, Deems Taylor, and Daniel Gregory Mason. The best of these composers, Loeffler, Carpenter, and Griffes, showed by their excellence that the tradition of technical competence in American art music established by Paine, Parker, Chadwick, and MacDowell would continue.

The musical devices employed by the American impressionists also reveal how up to date Americans were with regard to the latest developments in Europe. In his Violin Sonata (1911) Carpenter, like Debussy, made use of whole tone progressions and the high notes of the overtone series. In *Adventures in a Perambulator* (1914) he sought, like Ravel, musically to depict the world through the eyes of an infant. Thus he stated themes and, like a child, abruptly dropped them, never developing them maturely. Like many impressionists, Carpenter also referred to Iberian idioms in his Concerto for Piano and Orchestra, toyed with open fourth and fifth chords and with tonal clusters, and ended sections without tonic resolution.

Like their French contemporaries, Griffes and Loeffler, in addition to employing such devices as those Carpenter used, were interested in melodic progressions and harmonic suspensions that bordered on the chromatic. In his last works, Piano Sonata and *The Pleasure Dome of Kubla Khan* (both 1920), Griffes's music at times became completely atonal. Griffes and Loeffler were also fond of expressive instrumental combinations which created unusually translucent tone colors, seen, for example, in the passages for harp, oboe, and celesta in "The White Peacock" from Griffes's *Roman Sketches* (1915). In his Poem for Flute and Orchestra (1918) Griffes further complemented his general translucence in tonality and instrumental color by writing mostly in 9/8 time, discarding another traditional musical anchor, that of a clearly discernible pulse. In Griffes's Poem and in Loeffler's *Pagan Poem* (for piano and orchestra), the American impressionists also illustrated their indebtedness to the modern French innovators in their treatment of the solo instrument. In both works the soloist had to merge into the tone color scheme of the whole orchestra and, in contrast with Romantic works of this genre, avoid too much solo virtuosity.

The subject matter on which the impressionists based some of their works seemed rather decadent and risqué. (Griffes's *Pleasure Dome of Kubla Khan* drew from Coleridge's "Kubla Khan"; Loeffler's *Pagan Poem* was based on the eighth eclogue of Virgil, in which a Thessalian sorceress attempts to use her magical powers to draw back her departed lover.) Yet American music critics offered less opposition to impressionists than they had to earlier "musical anarchists" like Wagner, to such contemporaneous "anarchists" as Arnold Schoenberg, or to American vernacularists. Unfavorable criticism of impressionism was largely technical. To these critics, contrapuntal interest had to be present if a composer intended to follow his exposition with a development section. The critics were so closely tied to nineteenth-century norms of melody and development that they missed the impressionists' point.

Social criticism of the impressionists objected to their bohemian life style, a criticism which in Debussy's case was utterly false.[14] But even if it had been true, such a charge was milder than that of "anarchy." The latter applied to an individual interested in the negation of all rules governing composition; bohemianism implied only a shabbiness of life style and an indifference to social values and mores. Bohemianism was decadent; "musical anarchy" revolutionary. Revolutionaries wanted to blow up the concert hall; unwashed bohemians merely made it smell. Since bohemians constituted a less fundamental threat to society, their music could be heard with greater indulgence. Indeed, an impressionist like Debussy did present a milder threat to traditional tonality than did Schoenberg. Debussy expanded the tonal palette; Schoenberg seemed intent on throwing it on the junk heap. Debussy and his American counterparts thus became mildly acceptable to critics, and as the bohemian image faded, impressionism became ever more palatable.

Henry T. Finck, for example, while stating his personal disdain for Debussy's music, recognized that some *might* like it and recommended them to turn to "M. Loeffler of Boston."[15] Loeffler, a composer in the Debussian style, was also first desk violinist for the Boston Symphony Orchestra from 1882 to 1903 and a teacher at the New England Conservatory of Music. The New England Conservatory and the Boston Symphony were no havens for bohemians; they were the epitome of respectability. As Loeffler enjoyed personal favor in the proper critical circles, his music, along with Griffes's and Carpenter's, was tolerated.

Curiously, the fact that Loeffler was not native born enhanced his respectability and further explains why Finck deemed him acceptable. Loeffler, born in Mulhausen, Alsace, grew up near Kiev in the Ukraine and received his musical training in harmony and violin in Berlin and Paris. He came to Boston in 1881. His Paris and Berlin backgrounds lent polish that New York and Boston could hardly match, and his Ukrainian years added a touch of exoticism. There was nothing wrong with the critics' concerns for exoticism and polish, as both can stimulate good art, but it was odd how eclectically these concerns guided them. Polish could only come from Europe. Thus a composer had, by definition, to be European trained. Exotic materials such as Ukrainian elements were acceptable, but the indigenous American materials in the music of Dvořák and Burleigh were not. In painting, Americans of the French impressionist style like Mary Cassatt and John Singer Sargent gained entree into major museums and galleries while such contemporaries as Robert Henri, George Bellows, and John Sloan, whose subject matter was too "everyday," did not. Similarly, Loeffler had the entree to the concert halls of the United States; Burleigh never got in.

By 1910, then, there had been a shift in American art music away from the symphonic tradition of Schumann and Brahms. The French impressionists were rising, with rumblings of Americanism heard below.

The waning of German influence and the increasing acceptability of French impressionism in music and painting were part of a more general shift in American culture. In diplomacy, for example, German-American relations steadily deteriorated from 1890 to 1917. American disgust with the jingoistic militarism of the Kaiser contributed, as did the unashamedly Anglophilic views of leaders like Theodore Roosevelt, Henry Cabot Lodge, and John Hay. Through their efforts relations with England were strengthened and relations with Germany, England's greatest rival, were weakened. In the late nineteenth century English-French relations had evolved from torpor to the climax of the Entente Cordiale of 1904. With England and France now close, the United States also moved toward France diplomatically. Simultaneously, trade between the United States and France grew quickly after 1890, drawing the two closer together commercially as well.

Both the United States and England were disturbed by the political instability of France. The menace of Louis Napoleon and, for Americans, of Maximilian had been considerable. The threat of the Paris Commune aroused fearful attention internationally. During the unstable Third Republic, fears never subsided of France's devolution into monarchism, fears which were intense during the Boulanger crisis of 1888-1891. The Third Republic also received a bad press from its close ties with czarist Russia. All of these fears came to a head with the Dreyfus Affair. Then the situation changed. Dreyfus was exonerated, Boulanger failed in his attempt to take control of France, and by 1910 the political right in France was all but dead. Its collapse served to strengthen ties with England and the United States, which reached their height during World War I.

Political developments, of course, had little direct impact on the arts, but the parallel is important with regard to that essential group to the arts, the audience. Earlier French political instability was frightening Americans at the same time that they were confronting the challenges of musical anarchy and proletarianism. Thus in the 1870s and 1880s French Wagnerians like Gounod, Franck, and Saint-Saëns ran afoul of critics in American music centers. Bizet's *Carmen* (1875), with its lower-class subject matter, was also shocking. But by 1900, when France was more stable and democratic, Debussy and Ravel encountered less invective from critics and audiences.

While growing closer commercially and diplomatically, the French and Americans developed common intellectual interests in painting, music, and other fields as well. In 1904 French university professors began presenting lectures on American civilization. The *Nouvelle Revue Française,* founded in 1908, was organized for the purpose of revealing a France not identified with right-wing politics, antisemitism, or monarchism. The editors were also interested in American culture; they asked Waldo Frank, for example, to write an account of it for young French readers.[16] Shortly thereafter Pierre de Lanux, a young French writer, traveled in the United States and wrote several accounts, later published in book form as *Young France and New America.*[17] Identifying the "common principles" of democracy, he advocated that the two nations should work together in international ventures, so that these "principles," and not those of Prussian militarism, could be exported to underdeveloped areas.[18] In the same period, 1885 to 1920, several books by Americans appeared that dealt with French ways and culture: W. C. Brownwell, *French Traits* (New York: Charles Scribner's Sons, 1889); Barrett Wendell, *The France of Today* (New York: Charles Scribner's Sons, 1908); Rollin Lynde Hartt, *Understanding the French* (New York: McBride, Hart, and Co., 1914); and Edith Wharton, *French Ways and Their Meaning* (New York: D. Appleton, 1919). Though superficial, their tone was generally admiring.

Also at this time appeared some important writings by Americans on music history commenting favorably on French composers, the most important of which were written by Edward Burlingame Hill and Daniel Gregory Mason. Both were teachers (Hill at Harvard, Mason at Columbia) and composers in the impressionist style, as well as scholars. Hill wrote music reviews for the *Boston Transcript* and lectured on music history at Harvard from 1908 until 1942. In both capacities he always expressed great sympathy for the latest music of France. At Harvard, Hill expanded the music history curriculum, showing his predilections. In 1908 he offered a course on Brahms, Tchaikovsky, and Franck, removing Tchaikovsky in 1913. In 1910 he added a course entitled "D'Indy, Fauré, and Debussy," which included treatment of Chabrier, Charpentier, Dukas, and Ravel. Hill's courses, plus one on Beethoven, constituted the advanced-level music history curriculum at Harvard until 1924, illustrating a de-emphasis of the German Romantics. Beethoven could have been taught as an early Romantic, but to Hill and his generation of music historians, Beethoven represented the late phases of Classicism. This was the time of the first wave of scholarship, in which Hill played an important part, negating the glorification of Beethoven as the first Romantic composer—the man who freed music. Along these lines, Hill could also present Brahms as a composer who considered himself the upholder of the classical style versus the destructive challenge of Romanticism. In Chabrier, Franck, d'Indy, Fauré, Dukas, and Charpentier, Hill presented examples of French Wagnerians who, though greatly influenced by Wagner, departed from Wagnerian methods in imaginative ways, and he later emphasized this distinction in *Modern French Music,* published in 1924. Ravel and Debussy of course represented further imaginative steps away from German norms. It is not coincidence that many of the young American composers who lived in Paris in

the twenties—Virgil Thomson, Roger Sessions, Walter Piston—
were Harvard graduates and former pupils of Hill.

Daniel Gregory Mason's work at Columbia was similar. He joined
the Columbia faculty in 1905 and remained until 1942. In the
summer of 1913 he went to France to study composition with
Vincent d'Indy, and subsequently he taught methods of French
orchestration to his Columbia students.[19] Columbia was smaller
than Harvard, and no specialized music history courses existed,
only surveys, so that Mason's views are not so openly reflected
in the curriculum as Hill's. But his affinity for the French is clear
in his books. In an early work, *From Grieg to Brahms*, Mason wrote
most enthusiastically of Camille Saint-Saëns, and contrasting the
French master with such German contemporaries as Richard
Strauss, he emphasized "the service he [Saint-Saëns] does for
music by insisting on articulateness in feeling, logic in development,
and punctilious finese in workmanship."[20] In a later work, *Contemporary Composers*, which he employed as a text for his history
courses at Columbia, Mason showed his anti-German, pro-French
tastes:

> Apart from their gorgeous orchestral dress, [Strauss's]
> themes are with few exceptions commonplace, dull, and
> pretentious. . . . Disciples of the extensive or quantitative
> method [Mahler, Bruckner, and Strauss] aim to dazzle,
> stun, bewilder, and overwhelm. They can be recognized
> by their abuse of the brass and percussion groups, their
> childlike faith that if noise is only loud enough it be-
> comes noble.[21]

Mason was being overly harsh here, for no composer understood
the brass and exploited its capabilities better than Strauss. But
Mason's views were clear, and abundantly so to his students. While
flailing away at the Germans, he continued to extol the French,
particularly Debussy. He spoke admiringly of Debussy's music: "Its
dramatic directness, its justice of declamation, its moderation and
avoidance of Wagnerian exaggeration, perhaps above all . . . the
originality of its harmonic style and its delicately tinted orchestration."[22] Debussy, Mason said, "prefers innuendo, implication, and

understatement to the gross exaggeration of Strauss, the vehemence and platitude of Mahler, and the plodding literalism of Reger."[23] Both Mason and Hill played down the innovativeness of early twentieth-century German masters by classifying their new ideas as mere extensions (overextensions) of existing formulae. Both were far more excited about recent developments in France, saw the decline of Wagner's influence in French music as the takeoff point for the French, and thus implied a recommendation for an independent course for American music.

Similar developments took place in other music schools. New teachers such as Seth Bingham and Bruce Simonds at Yale and Gabriel Ysaye at the Cincinnati Conservatory of Music were more Francophilic in their musical tastes than their German-trained predecessors. Under such influences students increasingly preferred French schools over German ones for graduate training, a trend which began before the Great War and continued after it. Despite this shift, however, some disdain remained for the so-called lower genres of music. Horatio Parker and Henry Finck still had followers; the idea of music at an academic institution fell far short of common acceptance; and elitist postures by music educators were still normal.

None of the nation's major music schools, whether university-affiliated departments or independent conservatories, taught any of the rising popular genres in American music. Seeing their use, Daniel Gregory Mason showed a clear bias when he commented: "It is strange and somewhat repulsive to see European musicians, with a long and intensive culture behind them, at the behest of tired nerves throwing it all away and acclaiming American ragtime, the sweepings of our streets, as the rejuvenator of their senile art."[24]

The gap between vernacularism and art music still remained among leading American art music figures. It was left for the next generation, the first born in the twentieth century, to try to bridge this gap. One way was to forget the cultivated tradition, or at least its pedagogical institutions. But that meant less technical training. Indeed, this was a problem among many early twentieth-century Americanists. As Aaron Copland wrote of Henry Gilbert, "the fact is that he lacked the technique and musicianship for expressing his ideas in a significant way. . . . There is nothing . . . in a melody of folk source that cannot be effectively spoiled by a poor setting."[25] In addition to technical shortcomings, perhaps because of them, most early twentieth-century Americanists tended to cling to the older symphonic styles of Chadwick, Parker, and Paine. With regard to technique and musicianship, Gilbert and Farwell did not equal Griffes, Loeffler, or Carpenter. The best artist is at once technically competent, imaginative, and informed on the latest trends. Imagination is a given, but technical competence and up-to-date knowledge are more under individual control. For technique, musicians went to the best teachers and schools available, which in America as of 1920 meant Harvard and Columbia, where students were exposed to the latest developments in Western art music, with a decided French bias. For the final phases of technical training and in order to witness new trends at first hand, Americans went to Paris.

While wishing to be more capable than Gilbert and Farwell, American composers of the postwar generation shared their excitement about "American" music. But, as Aaron Copland recalled,

> We were after bigger game. Our concern was not with the quotable hymn or spiritual; we wanted to find a music that would speak of universal things in a vernacular of American speech and rhythms. We wanted to write on a level that left popular music far behind —music with a largeness of utterance wholly representative of the country Whitman had envisaged.[26]

For meeting all the needs—technical competence, modernity, and self-identity—the music world of Paris filled the bill.

NOTES

1. From one of MacDowell's lectures at Columbia University, quoted in Lawrence Gilman, *Edward MacDowell* (New York: John Lane Co., 1908), pp. 17-18.
2. Copland, *Music and Imagination*, p. 101.
3. Merton Robert Aborn, "The Influence on American Musical Culture of Dvořák's Sojourn in America" (Ph.D. diss., Indiana University School of Music, 1965), p. 175.

AMERICANISM AND FRENCH IMPRESSIONISM   29

4. "Dvořák Leads the Music Hall," *New York Herald*, October 22, 1892, p. 6.

5. Aborn, "Dvořák in America," p. 118.

6. *New York Herald*, December 17, 1893, p. 7.

7. *New York Tribune*, January 13, 1894, p. 7.

8. *New York Herald*, May 21, 1894, p. 28.

9. *New York Herald*, January 23, 1894, pp. 10-11.

10. Philip Hale, "The Kniesel Quartet Plays Dvořák's New Quartet," *Boston Journal*, January 2, 1894, p. 18.

11. Philip Hale, "Symphony of a Homesick Genius," *Boston Journal*, June 30, 1907, p. 17.

12. Henry T. Finck, *My Adventures in the Golden Age of Music* (New York: Funk and Wagnalls Co., 1926), p. 280.

13. Ibid., p. 279.

14. James Gibbons Huneker, *New York Sun*, July 19, 1903.

15. Henry T. Finck, *New York Post*, March 22, 1907.

16. Waldo Frank, *Our America* (New York: Boni and Liveright, 1919), passim; see also Warren Susman, "Pilgrimage to Paris" (Ph.D. diss., University of Wisconsin, 1958), p. 113.

17. Pierre de Lanux, *Young France and New America* (New York: Macmillan Co., 1917), passim.

18. Ibid., pp. 63-91.

19. Virgil Thomson, *American Music Since 1910* (New York: Holt, Rinehart and Winston, 1971), p. 5.

20. Daniel Gregory Mason, *From Grieg to Brahms: Studies in Some Modern Composers and Their Art* (Boston: Outlook Co., 1902), p. 120.

21. Daniel Gregory Mason, *Contemporary Composers* (New York: Macmillan Co., 1918), pp. 13-14, 17-18.

22. Ibid., p. 136.

23. Ibid.

24. Daniel Gregory Mason, *The Dilemma of American Music and Other Essays* (New York: Macmillan Co., 1928), p. 140.

25. Copland, *Music and Imagination*, p. 110.

26. Ibid., p. 111.

3 PARIS AND NEOCLASSICISM

With the Great War, France displaced Germany as the primary
foreign influence in American musical composition and pedagogy.
In the decade after the war virtually all young American composers
born between 1890 and 1910 went to Paris. George Antheil, Ernest
Bacon, Samuel Barlow, Robert Russell Bennett, Marc Blitzstein,
Radie Britain, Harold Brown, Mark Brunswick, Elliott Carter,
Theodore Chanler, Avery Claflin, Aaron Copland, Charles Cush-
ing, Robert Delany, Richard Donovan, John Duke, Herbert Elwell,
Ross Lee Finney, Isadore Freed, George Gershwin, Richard Ham-
mond, Howard Hanson, Roy Harris, Frederick Hart, John Haus-
sermann, Walter Heffer, Irwin Heilner, Mary Howe, Harrison
Kerr, Clair Leonard, Norman Lockwood, Otto Luening, Quinto
Maganini, Harl McDonald, Carl McKinley, Douglas Moore,
Walter Piston, Quincy Porter, Bernard Rogers, Robert Sanders,
Roger Sessions, Harrington Shortall, Elie Siegmeister, Leo Sowerby, Alexander Steinert, Howard Swanson, Louise Talma, Randall
Thompson, Virgil Thomson, Joseph Wagner, Max Wald, Powell
Weaver, and Adolph Weiss all spent some time there. For most the
stay was short, twelve months or less, but many stayed several
years. Two, Virgil Thomson and George Antheil, remained in
Paris for many years, associating with the Left Bank literati. Americans went to Paris for many individual reasons, but primarily to
study and experience at first hand the great artistic traditions both
past and present.

A major attraction of Paris was its general intellectual excitement.
Paris was the cosmopolitan crossroads of the artistic world. Scores

of artists from many cultures gathered there to work, to socialize, to argue, to learn, creating a brilliant efflorescence of arts. There has never been, before or since, a city for the arts like Paris in the twenties, and Americans came in flocks. The city was also a good working environment. To the Parisians, wrote Gertrude Stein, "foreigners were not romantic, they were just facts, nothing was sentimental, they were just there." Parisians' "simple clarity in respect to seeing life as it is, the animal and social life in human beings as it is" made for a refreshing, if at times intimidating, objectivity among Parisian critics and audiences.[1] Janet Flanner, Paris correspondent for the *New Yorker* in the twenties, explained why this environment was so attractive to Americans: it was a time and location in which the arts dominated one's thoughts. A certain ambivalence in Paris left artists to turn to themselves for support. They lived in select areas of the city, developed friendships and artistic circles, and often collaborated in work. Social and political matters were not important; the arts were. For the first time Americans were in close contact with others startlingly preoccupied with interests which, back home, were usually peripheral. Since Americans had few ethnic bonds in France, to experience Paris was to be, Flanner pointed out, at once thrust into the center of Western culture yet totally taken out of oneself.[2] You could test yourself and your worth. You could get sincere responses to your art. For American musicians this environment was part of the attraction. And Paris also had some great music teachers, as we shall see.

In addition to being open and objective, Paris was inexpensive. Two thousand dollars did nicely for a year there. To American musicians this figure was important, for the recently established Guggenheim Foundation supported many Americans with grants for that very amount. It would not have lasted six months in New York, but in Paris it provided a comfortable year, with plenty of wine. Economic conditions favored Paris over Germany or Austria. Americans visited these countries, but setting up home base in Berlin or Vienna was risky. In the early twenties neither economy was good; it was dangerous to change dollars into marks, and basics like food were often in short supply. There was nothing of this sort to worry about in Paris. As Virgil Thomson wrote, "I figured I may as well starve where the food is good."[3]

The most common reason for the travels of American composers was formal study. Study requires residence in one locale for a substantial length of time. In addition to instability in Germany and Austria, musical traditions were in flux. In Vienna the major developments were the innovations of Arnold Schoenberg, who in the early twenties had not yet fully systematized his 12-tone techniques. By the end of the decade he and his two major pupils, Anton Webern and Alban Berg, had systematized the innovations into the serial style, and at that point Americans began going to Vienna. Few went before. A similar situation existed vis-à-vis Germany. Viable music traditions certainly existed there. Kurt Weill and Paul Hindemith were gaining strong reputations, and Richard Strauss was still active. But Strauss represented the old Germany, the cultural nationalism extending back to Wagner, a musical tradition as hard to embrace as the politics of the Kaiser. Weill, like his contemporaries in Vienna, was just beginning his work. From the time he established himself, by the late twenties, he attracted Americans, and he continued to do so until the Nazis drove him out, to settle in New York, where he was influential until his death in 1950. Hindemith represented the tradition of German music most attractive to Americans—the lineage of Schumann and Brahms, the largely anationalistic wing of nineteenth-century German music, the extension of the threads of the Classical style against the destructive challenges of Romanticism and personal expressionism. These interests placed Hindemith in close affinity with contemporaries in Paris, the center of the Neoclassical world of which Hindemith was a part. He spent much of his time there, and Americans interested in modern styles of composition went there too.

The Neoclassical school of Paris, then, appeared, for social, financial, political, and esthetic reasons, the best place for study, and Americans came in droves. Neoclassicism marked a shift away from various tenets of the Romantic and Impressionist styles that had been dominant at the turn of the century. At that time symphonic, choral, and operatic works were generally longer than in earlier periods. Instrumental texture was thicker, as composers sought new nuances of tonal color. And composers like Wagner, Mahler, and Strauss emphasized the concept of composition as a vehicle for the expression of philosophy, not merely as a set of musical tones. By the decade after the Great War, a reaction had set in. Many composers felt that all these ideas had gone too far: pieces like the late symphonies of Mahler seemed too vast, the lush textures of Scriabin and Delius excessive. Philosophical expressions in music had reached the point of indulgent personalism. Wagner, for example, felt a listener should devote a day to contemplation before attending one of his music dramas. Such concern with philosophical expression had emerged as the status of the composer grew amidst the intellectual community. Before the mid-eighteenth century, music, other than that written for the church, had performed a largely decorative function, and the intellectual status of a composer was closer to a cook's than a philosopher's. In the nineteenth century music assumed a higher status, equal with that of the other arts, and composers developed as part of the intellectual community, not merely as craftsmen. But musicians after the Great War felt their predecessors' assertion of worth as intellectuals needed counterweight; there was a bit of truth in the eighteenth-century distinction, if not in the accompanying value judgment, between music and philosophy. In the twenties, composers, secure in their place among the arts, unashamedly pursued music as decorators, entertainers, or craftsmen. Neoclassicists like Stravinsky, Ravel, Poulenc, Milhaud, Satie, Rieti, Casella, Auric, Durey, Prokofiev, Shostakovich, Britten, Hindemith, Sessions, Finney, Copland, Harris, Carter, Piston, and Thomson all turned away from the evocative, earnest, lush indulgences of the turn of the century and pursued instead a more detached, restrained style with sharp melodic lines and overtly exact rhythms. They focused on smaller media, on horizontal elements (melody and rhythm) over vertical (harmony, texture, instrumentation), and on absolute music, music lacking in overt programmatic content. And they expressed themselves in what Stravinsky called "a precise and firm language stripped of all pictorial embellishments."[4]

Such were the main characteristics of Neoclassical music. Composers avoided the personalism, the excretions of ego they saw in their predecessors, and concentrated on more purely musical tasks. They bypassed many tenets of their immediate predecessors, resurrecting such eighteenth-century masters as J. S. Bach, Couperin, Rameau, Pergolesi, Haydn, and Mozart, in whom they found examples for many of their concerns. Thus they hopped over much of nineteenth-century music, reasserting in musical form and esthetic philosophy the long-ignored view of musical composition

as essentially an expression of tones, which at times can even be humorous. Stravinsky reflected the vigor of this reassertion when he said: "Epochs which immediately precede us are temporarily farther away from us than others which are more remote in time."[5] Indeed, in technique Neoclassicism marked a continuation of nineteenth-century developments, particularly in harmony, and here the Neoclassicists were closer to the Romantics and the Impressionists than they thought. Technically Neoclassicism marked merely an evolutionary step from the past. The harmonic language and rhythmic innovations extended the chromaticism and complexity of the music of the late nineteenth century, but the forms were those of the eighteenth. Within those forms, however, Neoclassicists did not reassert the order and symmetry of the music of that age. Theirs was a controlled eclecticism—classical forms with modern treatment. The models of the eighteenth century, coupled with the harmonic innovations of the twentieth, offered a myriad of musical possibilities.

The motives that led Neoclassicism were also varied. For two of the most famous and influential of its composers, Igor Stravinsky and Maurice Ravel, the motives were highly personal. Stravinsky had arrived on the musical scene of Paris before the rise of Neoclassicism. His early ballets—*Firebird* (1910), *Petrouchka* (1911), and *Le Sacre du Printemps* (1913)—were shatteringly innovative in regard to harmony and evoked violent reactions. But these works, tied in various ways to Russian music and folk traditions, marked a continuation of nineteenth-century Russian musical nationalism. Stravinsky was the greatest Russian composer of the generation that developed in the wake of the conscious nationalism of the so-called Group of Five—Mussorgsky, Cui, Borodin, Balakirev, and Rimsky-Korsakov, whose pupil he was. His three great ballets, like other early works, marked the climax of this musical nationalism. The onset of the Great War fueled Stravinsky's nationalism, but as it dragged on he grew disenchanted, and nationalism seemed increasingly naive. His disenchantment led him, as a composer, from national expressions toward a language devoid of trappings, more concerned with musical tones. In this creative avenue he felt at ease, and he stayed there.

With the February/March revolution of 1917 Stravinsky's nationalism was further weakened. Like many artists, Stravinsky was generally apolitical. He had had little to do with political events while in Russia, and in the West he kept abreast of events but did nothing more. Support of the Tsar was simply a matter of habit, and the Tsar's abdication left him neither shocked nor outraged but simply lost. His reaction to the Bolshevik takeover further illustrates his distance from political events. At first he made no comment of any sort about the Bolsheviks in his *Autobiography*. Only gradually, as the Soviets slowly extended their control of the arts, did he become embittered and speak out. His chief concern in 1917 was financial, as he was now cut off from many of his resources. His financial difficulties coincided with those of the Ballet Russe, for which he did much of his writing. With a general lack of funding, no longer would the Ballet Russe and Stravinsky stage large-scale ballets like *Le Sacre du Printemps*. (And in addition to financial problems, their major dancer, Vaslav Nijinsky, had gone insane.) There was little point in Stravinsky's writing any more grand pieces, and he turned to smaller ones.

Among the notable new works that subsequently emerged were *L'Histoire d'un Soldat* (1918) and *Pulcinella* (1919). *L'Histoire d'un Soldat* illustrated the musical quality Stravinsky could develop in small ensemble writing. The scenario—a Faustian theme of a soldier forsaking responsibility, falling prey to the worldly charms of the devil—demonstrated a turn to anationalistic subject matter. *Pulcinella*, derived from fragments of works by the eighteenth-century Neapolitan composer Giovanni Pergolesi, represented Stravinsky's first clear turn to the music of that era. Working on the score, Stravinsky wrote, he came to "appreciate more and more the true nature of Pergolesi while discerning ever more clearly the closeness of my mental and, so to speak, sensory kinship with him."[6] He developed a musical style that would mark his work for the next twenty-five years. Pablo Picasso collaborated with Stravinsky on this ballet (he designed the stage settings and costumes), and Stravinsky was delighted with Picasso's work here and elsewhere. Their relationship provided a mutual reinforcement of their respective shifts to Neoclassicism.*

Stravinsky was now an exile from Russia, both physically and

---

*For a few years, 1918 to 1923, Picasso shifted away from abstractionism and cubism. With such works as *Trois Femmes à la Fontaine*, *La Source*, *Flute de Pan*, *Trois Grâces*, and portraits of his wife, his son (there were many of these), Jean Cocteau, and Igor Stravinsky, he leaned to more realistic, classical renderings of the human form.

financially. He spoke little French and even less English, which increased his malaise. But he "spoke" the language of musical notation, and in eighteenth-century music this language held center stage. The early ballets had revealed the composer's affinity for modern techniques. Like most modernists, Stravinsky had encountered much harsh criticism, a good deal of it amounting to little more than sweeping indictments of modern decadence: more serious was the question of whether his innovations constituted a sharp break or a logical progression from past standards. Critics asked if Stravinsky could work within traditional forms. Wagner had often received criticism along these lines and had silenced his critics with *Die Meistersinger von Nürnberg* (1867). Picasso's Neo-classical interlude was, in part, similarly motivated. Stravinsky clearly knew the present; so as not to be dismissed as a hypermodernist, he needed to prove that he knew the past. *L'Histoire, Pulcinella,* and others provided the proof, and this led his style and study to the eighteenth century, as well as to different parts of his Russian musical past. Earlier he had presented himself as the successor to the nationalism of the Five; in the twenties he separated himself from that. Some of his new music was absolute, like the *Octet* (1923), or anationalistic *(L'Histoire),* but other compositions were based on Russian themes—*Mavra* (1922), *Le Rossignol* (1917), *The Fairy's Kiss* (1928), and *Chanson Russe* (1937)—and the *Capriccio* (1929) and *Symphony of Psalms* (1930) contain bits of Russian themes as well. To preserve his linguistic and personal identity Stravinsky needed to remain identifiably Russian. Historically *Mavra, The Fairy's Kiss,* and *Chanson Russe* reveal the influence of a certain segment of the Russian musical past, not that of the Five but that of Mikhail Glinka and, even more, of Tchaikovsky. *Mavra,* written for Serge Diaghilev's Ballet Russe, was an adaptation of Tchaikovsky's *Sleeping Beauty.* In reaction some critics commented on the relatively old-fashioned style of Stravinsky's music.[7] He was not surprised. His shift had been deliberate. The Tchaikovsky "branch" of nineteenth-century Russian music, in opposition to the Five, stood in disfavor in official Soviet circles on the grounds that it was allegedly more cosmopolitan, more bourgeois, more influenced by contemporaneous developments in the West, and more favored by the Romanov court. On the matter of foreign influences, Stravinsky commented:

It is true that Tchaikowsky could not escape Germanic influences. But, though he was under the influence of Schumann, that did not prevent him from remaining Russian any more than Gounod . . . was prevented from remaining French. Both profited by the purely musical discoveries of the great German, who was himself so eminently a musician [as opposed, for example, to Wagner, so eminently a cultural nationalist]. They borrowed his phraseology and his distinctive idioms without adopting his ideology.[8]

Stravinsky had emerged from the more overt nationalism of the Five. After 1917-1918, as a break with a Russia cut off and co-opted by political forces he increasingly disliked, he needed to transcend that past yet still remain identifiably Russian. Glinka and Tchaikovsky, accompanying a lean, Neoclassical language, provided a means that gave balance against developments in the Soviet Union and an anchor during commerce with Western European traditions.

For Americans Stravinsky was the most famous composer in Paris. His music, by mere example, had great influence. Moreover, he was very close to Nadia Boulanger. He habitually showed her scores, which she sometimes used as pedagogical examples for her American pupils. For Americans this lent a sense of being terribly *à la page* and further enhanced the lure of Stravinsky's musical style.

While a complex network of factors, musical, personal and political, motivated Stravinsky's turn to Neoclassicism, Maurice Ravel's changes after 1917 were more purely personal. Ravel abandoned the lush, texturally thick orchestration of his impressionist years. He had shown tendencies toward the leaner Neoclassical style early in his career, in, for example, *Minuet Antique* (1895), and concise, lucid forms always seemed more congenial to his reticent nature. His unmatched ability at orchestration, however, permitted him to color subsequent works with an impressionist hue. But his predilections remained for, and his best work was in, miniature forms. His masterful orchestration, like his life style as a connoisseur, was a lovely mask for innocent, childlike sensibilities, revealed in the subject matter—toys, children, witches, music boxes, fairy tales—of his most successful programmatic works.* Never did Ravel strive tonally for extramusical expression, only for tones, with occasional fantasies as thematic bases. After his mother died in 1917 he never regained his earlier precocious thematic content. In 1919 he wrote: "I think of those former times when I was so happy. . . . It will soon be three years since mother died, and my despair increases from day to day. . . . I no longer have this dear silent presence enveloping me with her tenderness, which was, I see it more clearly now than ever, my only reason for living."[9] Ravel wrote less frequently after this. Decreased interest in communicating his ideas led him first away from programmatic to absolute music. Like Stravinsky, Ravel had been separated from a spiritual source. Stravinsky, however, would continue to create in his new environment, while Ravel's difficulty in communication steadily increased. Even in the genre of absolute music he found no solace and wrote less and less. His malaise assumed physiological as well as psychological dimensions which physicians have never been able to diagnose. By 1934 he would write but a few letters and only then by copying each word from a dictionary. He died in 1937.

Like Stravinsky, Ravel provided Americans with musical examples of the highest order. Also like Stravinsky, Ravel appealed to Americans by his presence in Paris and his music's hot-off-the-press availability. Another source of his appeal was his power to encapsulate many of the tenets of Neoclassicism which Americans found relevant. Later Virgil Thomson explained that Ravel

> is not today, nor was he during his lifetime . . . a misunderstood composer. . . . his work presents fewer difficulties of comprehension than that of any of the other great figures of the modern movement. . . . Nobody could fail, nobody ever has failed to perceive at first sight what it [Ravel's music] is all about.
>
> What it is all about is a nonromantic view of life. Not an antiromantic view, simply a nonromantic one, as if the nineteenth century had never, save for its technical discoveries, existed.[10]

---

*The most successful interpretations of Ravel's music are those in which all technical problems, no matter how severe, are hidden by a pervading aura bordering on that of a child playing rudimentary exercises.

Neoclassicists like Thomson wanted to free themselves from nineteenth-century standards, not to show where nineteenth-century tenets were esthetically warped, not to poke fun at them, but simply to transcend them. In Ravel they saw how this could be done. The enthusiasm with which Thomson described the completely obvious bent of Ravel, despite the fact that his music continues to unveil many analytical questions, reveals the appeal of such a musical model.

Highly personal factors motivated Stravinsky's and Ravel's switch to Neoclassicism. These factors were of little direct relevance to the Americans studying in Paris. But the availability of the two men's music, their technical brilliance, and the aesthetic bases of their styles had great impact. The great differences between their styles furthered many possible means of Neoclassical expression. The influences of Stravinsky and Ravel, however, fully account neither for the impact of Neoclassicism on Americans nor for the appeal of Paris. The activities and sensibilities of other French composers greatly strengthened the appeal of Parisian Neoclassicism to Americans.

"We want our own music," proclaimed Erik Satie, "and if possible without the sauerkraut."[11] For the French, the nationalistic spirit of World War I heightened objections to a musical past tied to German, Romantic styles. Americans had undergone a similar, if less severe, war experience which touched their music world. American dependence on Germany had declined before the war, but its influence still remained. Then during the war there were anti-German episodes in the music world. Several prominent German musicians in the United States, the best known Karl Muck, conductor of the Boston Symphony Orchestra, were arrested and deported. Orchestras played much less German music than ever before, and the boycott continued after the war, as anti-German feelings slowly subsided.

Though the German influence faded, American composers, still needing to forge their own identity amidst European traditions, continued looking to Europe for guidance. As Virgil Thomson held, American music no longer needed a "German grandfather" but a "French big brother."[12] Concurrently the French were also turning away from vestiges of German domination. With that movement grew a desire for a usable past, not German influenced, distinctly French if possible. This drew composers like Satie and

Ravel to the late Baroque and Classical works of Couperin and Rameau. In order to demonstrate the contrast between themselves and their more German-influenced predecessors, Satie and his friends also cast aspersions on the Impressionists. A group of six composers—Darius Milhaud, Francis Poulenc, Arthur Honegger, Louis Durey, Georges Auric, and Germaine Taileferre—met with Satie in May 1917. Over the next ten years they met occasionally and propounded some general aims for the future of French music. "Les Six" was a loosely knit group. They seldom collaborated with one another and were united by only a few basic concerns: desire for objectivity in musical composition, opposition to music tied to German standards, and impatience with generally conservative musical tastes among audiences and critics. These concerns led them to use eighteenth-century French models with a lean musical language, devoid of the embellishments and trappings associated with the dominant styles of the late nineteenth century, and on these grounds they objected to the lush, sensuous music of the French Impressionists. Stravinsky and Ravel provided Americans with excellent musical examples, but Satie and Les Six provided musical ideas, appropriately loose, complete with anti-German political trappings, relevant to young Americans' concerns. The American composers felt they were forging new ground for themselves and for their nation's musical traditions. Among the French composers they found examples that suited their anti-German and technically modern orientation. Neoclassicism was part of this anti-German/modern picture for Stravinsky and the French. It became so for Americans.

The lean character of the musical language of Satie and Les Six conformed to the aesthetic precepts of another of the group's mentors—Jean Cocteau. Cocteau wrote of the need for directness of expression. Much as his American contemporary Ernest Hemingway, Cocteau opposed decorative writing. And as was the case with Hemingway, Cocteau's concerns took on a hypermasculine character. Art had developed, according to Cocteau and Hemingway, excessive civility. They compensated with consciously unornamented, at times primitive, manners of writing and living. Satie and Les Six added to this direct, uncomplicated music with great emphasis on linear melodic and rhythmic matters and comparatively little on such vertical properties as texture and instrumentation.

Satie and Les Six were, appropriately, among the early French enthusiasts for American jazz. In this France provided further intellectual support for Americans, as the interest in idioms like jazz underscored the lack of logic in the separation of vernacular and art music traditions, a separation which young American musicians increasingly opposed. Weaknesses in French uses of jazz also stimulated Americans. As Aaron Copland pointed out, only one French composer, Darius Milhaud, worked with jazz idioms in convincing ways.[13] Thus there were things Copland and his generation could teach their French "big brothers."

The French musicians' interest in jazz was part of a broader concern on their part for the exotic. A variety of music was readily available in Paris, a cosmopolitan city if there ever was one. In 1920 Parisians could hear performances of music indigenous to North Africa, West Africa, China, Southeast Asia, and the Pacific islands. Heitor Villa-Lobos brought to postwar Paris the music of his native Brazil. The Ballet Russe gave exposure to music of the modern Russians, Serge Prokofiev and Stravinsky. American jazz performers like Sidney Bechet, Josephine Baker, and Billy Arnold, and later Louis Armstrong and Paul Whiteman were very popular, and these Americans met few of the sneers previously extended to Dvořák and Burleigh. Parisian audiences displayed wider tastes, and French composers were fascinated by various exotic influences. West African modes, for example, greatly influenced Debussy, and West African rhythmic elements had a similar impact on Stravinsky. Ravel's *Asie* showed his interest in different Oriental scales, and Darius Milhaud's cycle for piano, *Saudades do Brazil*, showed similar interest in Latin-American idioms.

But the foreign elements that fascinated French musicians and audiences as much as any were American jazz and ragtime. Claude Debussy was the first to show this interest when he used ragtime figures in "Golliwog's Cake-Walk" from *The Children's Corner* (1908). For Debussy ragtime was primitive and simple, hence altogether appropriate in a children's corner. In "General Lavine," from the second book of Preludes for Piano, Debussy attempted musically to illustrate a man of eccentric character; the odd rhythms of ragtime suited his purposes nicely. In his consciously modern ballet *Parade* (1916), Satie used bits of jazz, along with pistol shots and typewriters, to symbolize modernity in contrast with traditional musical ways. Ernst Krenek, a Vienna-born Czech composer who spent much of his time in postwar Paris, employed jazz for similar effects in his opera *Jonny Spielt Auf* (1926). In *Le Boeuf sur la Toit* (1919), a ballet satirizing American prohibition, Darius Milhaud used jazz figures to embellish the theme of mockery. The speed of his response, as prohibition had just become law, illustrates the degree to which he and others were taking note of things American. Milhaud's most famous jazz piece was *La Création du Monde* (1923), perhaps the most successful use of jazz by any French composer. "Better than any European," recalled Aaron Copland, "Milhaud understood how to assimilate the jazz idiom."[14] Just as Milhaud learned Latin-American idioms for *Saudades do Brazil* by visiting Brazil, he learned his jazz by visiting clubs in Harlem in 1921 and 1922. His direct contact with both music and locale may explain his success, as well as others' shortcomings.

In *La Création du Monde* Milhaud depicted the creation of the world through a series of related motifs. In the beginning he presented a languid theme in the saxophone, juxtaposed with a more vibrant, jazz-like motif in the trumpet. This symbolized a peaceful world with hints of creative energy beneath. The jazz motif subsequently emerged in rhythmically altered and expanded form, presented first in the contrabass, forming the basis of a fugue, jazz-like with accents on points other than the first beat of a measure and with tonal elaboration on the accented notes. Here, then, Milhaud illustrated rising forces in the early stages of the world's creation through the idiom of jazz, which from his perspective was not terribly genteel or civilized. The next section of the piece is a refinement of the jazz motif, symbolizing the taming of the primitive. In the remainder of the work, with the languid, primitive, and civilized themes exposed, Milhaud developed different combinations of the three, demonstrating his conviction that creative development stems from an interaction of different forces. A most interesting aspect of the piece is its similarity in motif and instrumentation with George Gershwin's *Rhapsody in Blue*, written two years later. Gershwin, in his efforts to write symphonic jazz, encountered difficulties from critics who disapproved of attempts to unite so-called "high" and "low" art. Milhaud's earlier flirtation with such a concept indicates the favorable environment that Americans found in Paris. Milhaud and his French contemporaries revealed an open-minded attitude toward exotic musics, including jazz. Milhaud showed the high degree of sensitivity and understanding in France which subsequent French *and* American musicians would follow.

While Debussy, Satie, Krenek, and Milhaud had in mind specific musical and dramatic effects which American idioms abetted, other composers used jazz simply because it was new. George Auric, Igor Stravinsky, Maurice Ravel, and Arthur Honegger composed some jazz and blues-like music simply because they wanted to explore new rhythmic, tonal, intervallic, and harmonic potentialities.* Their efforts were not always successful. Auric captured fox trot rhythms, but harmonically his two-piano piece is full of arpeggiated seventh and ninth chords and sounds like an impressionist étude. Honegger only used touches of blues harmony in *Le Roi David*. In his Concertino he attempted to create a jazz aura only in the finale, merely through a percussive use of the piano, so his jazz, while not unsuccessful, was severely limited in scope. In his more ambitious Prelude and Blues he created jazz effects in rhythm and harmony. But his instrumentation—four chromatic harps—was utterly incongruous.

A contemporary reviewer called Stravinsky's American touches "neither ragtime fish nor jazz flesh."[15] Stravinsky's uses of jazz and ragtime in the twenties coincided with his turn in compositional style toward Neoclassicism. Now writing for small ensembles, Stravinsky found that the form of his *Ragtime* fitted his new interests. A primary characteristic of all of Stravinsky's music is its rhythmic ingenuity. Rhythm is also a primary ingredient in ragtime, but ragtime's interest arises from syncopation around a steady beat. Stravinsky's rhythmic genius lay in the terrific complexity of rhythmic elements. Consequently, in the *Ragtime* Stravinsky's own tendencies overwhelmed the relatively simple rhythmic character of ragtime. He piled syncopation upon syncopation, drowning all sense of clear rhythm, and hence any relation-

---

*American idioms—jazz, ragtime, or blues—are present in parts of the following works: *L'Enfant et les Sortilèges* (1924-25), *Violin Sonata*, second movement ("Blues") (1923-27), and *Piano Concerto* (1930), by Ravel; *Fox-Trot for Two Pianos* (1926), by Auric; Ragtime for Eleven Instruments (1920) and *L'Histoire du Soldat* (1918), by Stravinsky; and "Je fas conçu dans la péché" from *Le Roi David* (1921), Concertino for Piano and Orchestra (1924), and Prelude and Blues for Four Chromatic Harps (1925), by Honegger.

ship with ragtime. Similarly, with regard to thematic treatment Stravinsky was too intricate for his chosen form. Dissonances flitted in and out. He employed thematic disintegration and concertato principles, a rapid trading of themes from instrument to instrument, thus losing another ragtime element—the identity of the individual player. According to his later associate, Robert Craft, Stravinsky believed jazz was not essentially rhythmic but "a combination of hypnotic regularity in the beat and indulgent rubato in the melodies. This totally opposed Stravinsky's sense of 'ontological' time [his emphasis on carefully constructed meter as the basis of his music] and human responsibility for conscious order [which led to impatience with improvisation or with any similar sort of indulgence]. His interest in jazz centered on its sonorities rather than its rhythms."[16]

Maurice Ravel seemed better able to understand the relationship between syncopation and steady meter in jazz. Consequently the bits of jazz in the third movement of his Piano Concerto worked well. But as with Honegger, Ravel's use of jazz was limited here. In L'Enfant et les Sortilèges he employed jazz and fox trot motifs in combination with other elements, notably Chinese modes. Naturally, the jazz effect was strained, but Ravel meant it to be so. The combinations seems eclectic, but he was writing about a child and witches, so bizarre juxtapositions were logical. The second movement, "Blues," of his Violin Sonata, if it was an attempt at depicting the blues, was not altogether successful. Probably, however, Ravel merely wished to write a blues-like piece with some of the genre's harmonic and thematic characteristics. Some parts sound like blues; others do not. He wrote violin and piano parts in imitation of saxophone and guitar, but the resemblance between the two pairs is weak. The shifting irregular tonalities, differing not only between violin and piano, but between the right and left hand of the piano, create uneasiness rather than melancholia. Ravel began with a legitimate track for blues, with a monotonous four-four chordal section in the piano. But then he allowed the piano thematic passages, which was not out of character for blues, except that he did not subordinate the violin when he set the piano free. Thus the relationship between the parts became polyphonic, something out of character for a blues duet. When Ravel finally brought the violin to a subordinate position, he created some legitimate blues riffs. But this did not last very long, as he abruptly jumped into a long, rather bizarre variation of the first section, and in doing so created an obtuse version of the sonata form, certainly not a normal structure for blues. He did, however, end the piece on a seventh chord. Perhaps the primary characteristic of blues is the tonal relationship between the tonic, subdominant, and dominant (C, F, and G, for example, in the key of C). Sensitive to this, Ravel, was able to create blues harmonies, but not the blues. There were no traces of blue notes—a flatted submediant in the major mode (A flat in relationship to C, for example). More importantly, the harmony and rhythm, as with Stravinsky, were interesting, but too complex for blues. The piece gives no hint of the feeling of the players or of the composer. It is music of the intellect, not blues. It ain't funky. But, like Stravinsky, Ravel was probably not trying to write an actual blues piece suitable for the back streets of Memphis or St. Louis. He was merely having some fun with a genre new and fascinating to him.

French musicians' fascination with jazz was part of a general interest in exotic music, the creative products of little known and superficially less civilized cultures. Indeed, the most successful French uses of jazz, in Milhaud and Debussy, were in programs explicitly barbaric or childlike. The early twentieth-century French, of course, had none of the problems of race relations that existed in the United States to block their integration of black American idioms and Classical forms. In France, for example, blacks and whites could marry. (Of course, the plight of Moroccans and Algerians in France is another story, not unlike that of blacks in America. Generically speaking, the French have their own "niggers.") In both specific legislation and general social mores, black/white relations in France were generally more open than in the United States, and the French fascination with jazz reflected this. The French musicologists Hughes Panaissé and Robert Goffin were, furthermore, the first to study jazz, while American musicologists remained wedded to a vernacular/art music dichotomy. When the reputable journal *Revue Musicale* began reviewing records in 1926, as a matter of course jazz recordings were included; jazz was simply another part of music literature. Composers, too, used jazz simply because it was musically interesting.

French enthusiasm for jazz gave American idioms respectability.

As young Americans were arriving in Paris, the French music world was developing interest in things American. Considering the stature of Debussy, Ravel, and Stravinsky, Americans were heartened to pursue their own music without fear of being charged with musical anarchy or vulgarity. The stuffiest critic had to take note when Ravel remarked: "Jazz is a very rich and vital source of inspiration for modern composers, and I am astonished that so few Americans are influenced by it."[17] Ravel knew few of the Americans in Paris at the time he spoke. The French composers' general failure at emulating jazz further stimulated Americans to unite their vernacular and art music spheres. For they felt they could do it better.

Americans were both heartened and influenced by developments in the Paris intellectual and music world. They felt, if only vicariously, a sense of importance, since they represented a culture which so fascinated many of the music world's great figures. Paris was enticing. But the most important factor in the magnetism the city exerted on so many American composers was pedagogical. Virtually all Americans spent some time in formal study with one of two teachers—Nadia Boulanger and Vincent d'Indy.

It was not new for American composers to study in France. Gottschalk had done so, and so had MacDowell, the latter at the Paris Conservatoire, the most prestigious school in France up to 1890. As time went on, however, the Conservatoire seemed increasingly old fashioned. The ideal form of composition at the Conservatoire was opera. Its standards of writing stemmed from the ideals of the judges of the most prestigious composition award of the time, the Prix de Rome, and its professors held suspect any departures from these standards. Operatic ideals were largely Wagnerian, although by 1890 new international influences, notably from Russia, had grown. There was also a revival at the Conservatoire of interest in other past music: eleventh- and twelfth-century Gregorian chant, the Renaissance polyphony of Palestrina, the seventeenth-century opera of Monteverdi, the eighteenth-century French instrumental music of Couperin and Rameau, and the Classical forms of Haydn, Mozart, and Beethoven. Some teachers came to realize that a neglect of these traditions could hamper, perhaps ruin, a composer, particularly a student. Believing changes were in order for the methods of training composers, two men, César Franck and Vincent d'Indy, led a committee to develop a plan to reorganize the curriculum of the Conservatoire. In 1890 they recommended for students more general training in liberal arts and broader grounding in music history. The Conservatoire rejected the recommendations. Franck died in 1890, but d'Indy carried on the fight. He and his sympathizers, notably Charles Bordes and Alexander Guilmant, resigned from the Conservatoire and formed their own school in 1894, the Schola Cantorum; there they put their recommmendations into practice. D'Indy was the leading figure at the Schola Cantorum and remained so until his death in 1931.

To d'Indy's classes flocked many innovative musicians, among them such Americans as Daniel Gregory Mason, Arthur Farwell, Quincy Porter, and Harvey B. Gaul. During his tenure, d'Indy developed his *Cours de Composition*,[18] required reading for all composition students. In this massive work he presented a history of musical forms—fugue, suite, sonata, chamber music, string quartet, overture, symphony, concerto, symphonic poem, fantasie— from the third century A.D. to the present. He emphasized eleventh and twelfth-century Gregorian chant, the music of the late Renaissance and early Baroque, and non-German traditions of the eighteenth century. He took a dim view of nineteenth-century music, considering the age a "silly" period.[19] Like Ravel, then, d'Indy aided efforts to escape the shadow the nineteenth century cast on the twentieth. D'Indy's disdain for many of modern composers of his era, including Stravinsky, Bartók, and Schoenberg, sharpened his views on the "silliness" of the nineteenth century. The moderns, he felt, had become consciously avant-garde in trying to escape the immediate past. They had thus lost consciousness of history. They did not build on the past, they discarded it. d'Indy carried on the fight. He and his sympathizers, notably As a consequence of inadequate historical knowledge, he saw a gross misrepresentation of composers of the nineteenth century, notably Beethoven, who was regarded by composers and historians of the mid- and late nineteenth century as a Romantic. D'Indy, along with other scholars like Edward B. Hill at Harvard and Donald Francis Tovey in England, destroyed this image. Beethoven emerged, as did Goethe, Hegel, and Schubert, as a Classicist who worked within eighteenth-century forms and provided in his craft inklings of later Romantic developments. D'Indy saw a dislike of Beethoven among such contemporaries as Debussy, Dukas, and

Stravinsky and felt that both their taste and their avant-garde tendencies arose from a false historical sense. Accordingly, the treatment of Beethoven in the *Cours de Composition* emphasized his ties to other Classicists, particularly Haydn. D'Indy also devoted much attention to Frederick Wilhelm Rust (1735-1796), whom he saw as a technical precursor to Beethoven, albeit without Beethoven's imaginative genius. This emphasis on transitional figures underscored further the smooth evolutionary process d'Indy considered fundamental in music history.

In several letters to d'Indy, published in *Le Monde Musicale*, the composer Camille Saint-Saëns took him to task for this interpretation of Rust, which he felt to be a gross overstatement.[20] In keeping with his fastidious scholarly nature, d'Indy duly noted Saint-Saëns's criticism in his *Cours*. The debate over Rust was part of a more fundamental dispute between the two. Saint-Saëns felt that d'Indy attached too much significance to César Franck, who had been d'Indy's teacher at the Conservatoire. Franck and d'Indy had remained close thereafter and shared common compositional and pedagogical values. In the *Cours* d'Indy saw Franck as the final phase of European symphonic and choral traditions, just as he saw Wagner as the culmination of developments in programmatic music. On the other hand, Saint-Saëns felt that Franck was but one of many contemporaries who continued symphonic and choral traditions, and he saw far more significance in Franz Liszt and Richard Strauss, both of whom he felt d'Indy ignored.

While d'Indy and Saint-Saëns agreed fundamentally on the significance of Wagner in the development of programmatic music, the nature of Saint-Saëns's enthusiasm was different. D'Indy wrote that in the *Ring of the Nibelung* Wagner had become too concerned with epic poetry, ignoring theatrical action: "Wagner wished to establish a German epic poem; he . . . carried to it his genius and his exaggerations. . . . It is not the stage [but Wagner] which is preeminent in *Der Ring.*"[21] As shown in his own opera, *L'Etranger,* d'Indy believed a composer of opera should make philosophy a vehicle for musical and dramatic ideas. Wagner, he felt, had reversed this concept. In contrast, Saint-Saëns saw nothing wrong with Wagner's philosophical approach to music drama. Saint-Saëns thus understood and accepted the cultural nationalism that surrounded Wagner; d'Indy ignored it. With this contrasting sensitivity to cultural nationalism in Wagner and in other German composers, Saint-Saëns and d'Indy were at odds during World War I as to whether French orchestras should play German music. Saint-Saëns said no; d'Indy why not? Earlier, in November 1886, d'Indy and Franck had pushed a resolution through the Société Nationale that lifted the ban on foreign music at the Société concerts, a resolution that Saint-Saëns opposed and that prompted his resignation when it passed.

D'Indy could not accept the submission of music to any nonmusical themes, except religious ones. Thus to him nationalism was simply a nonissue in music; any such submission smacked of commercialism. The alleged devolution of art into commercialism, which d'Indy saw affecting such contemporaries as Massenet and Bizet, was an aspect of nineteenth-century music that prompted d'Indy's charge of silliness. One offshoot of this was that it strengthened D'Indy's right-wing political views. He was a monarchist, a follower of Charles Maurras and the *Action Française* and strongly antisemitic. He saw the decadent commercialism of French music as the responsibility of Jewish impressarios, who dragged French music institutions from artistic to business enterprises and brought with them Jewish composers like Meyerbeer, Offenbach, Halevy, Herold, and Auber.[22] In connection with Felix Mendelssohn he wrote: "Always skillful in appropriating the knowledge of others, the Jews are seldom true artists by nature."[23] But just as it is unfair to castigate the entire opus of Wagner because of his alleged proto-Nazism, it is simplistic to dismiss all of d'Indy's commentaries as mere antisemitic outcroppings. That he simplistically linked his legitimate musical concerns to hateful political ideologies reveals how contrastingly simple he was in politics, where he had little knowledge or training. Arnold Schoenberg pointed this out in 1945, in the wake of moves against musicians who at least collaborated with the Nazis: artists, he said, are "like immature children, [so] call them fools and let them escape."[24] D'Indy expressed genuine fear about the consequences of commercialization; an artist might cease following his ideas merely cater to popular taste, and thus become a "tailor" rather than a creator. Particularly as a pedagogue, such a prospect distressed him, and he determined to deflect his students from it.

D'Indy's pedagogical and compositional values stemmed from his religious faith. A devout Catholic, he believed that faith was an essential element in all great art. For this reason he was greatly distressed, after praising the oratorios of the contemporary opera composer Jules Massenet, to hear the composer respond: "Oh I don't believe in all that Jesus stuff, . . . but the public likes it, and we must always agree with the public."[25] Massenet had separated ethics from his aesthetics, removing any moral element from his work. This d'Indy could not tolerate. He believed art was born of religion, as only an act of God can explain artistic expression and genius. Thus as a teacher he accepted the fact that he could not create genius. "No artistic education," he wrote, "can bestow genius where it does not exist; but it can bring talent to birth and it must shape taste"[26] Shaping of taste and development of talent would come through rigorous study, and d'Indy's conceptions here were also tied to his religious faith. One contemporary puckishly wrote of his "medieval propensity for developing elaborate theories from unsound premises."[27] Whether or not his premises were sound, his *Cours de Composition* is indeed an elaborate, integrated series of pedagogical exercises designed to give students an organic conception of musical development.

Despite his disdain for those artistic attitudes that violated his sensibilities, d'Indy was always personally courteous to everyone. His religious background led him to dislike the Renaissance and Reformation, yet in the *Cours* he attached great importance to the Renaissance and early Baroque composer Claudio Monteverdi. The *Cours de Composition* and the Schola Cantorum could and did aid the development of students whose compositional styles d'Indy himself disliked. Georges Auric and Honegger were two of his noteworthy pupils. Both were interested in uniting technical innovations of past masters into modern forms. Compared with those of other contemporaries, their ideas seemed evolutionary rather than revolutionary, but their writings were more avant-garde than anything for which d'Indy cared. A yet more striking example of d'Indy's willingness to accommodate different musical personalities is the case of Erik Satie. Satie's bohemian manner was the antithesis of that of the impeccable d'Indy, and Satie's hypermodern compositional style, employing pistol shots and a typewriter in a ballet score, seemed decadent. Also he was openly contemptuous of German music. Since sensitivity to German domination prevailed among other French composers, like Saint-Saëns, it seems odd that such disdainful anti-Germanism as Satie's would emerge from d'Indy's classes. But, true to his basic courtesy, d'Indy never discouraged Satie from going in the personal or professional directions he chose. He considered that outside his duty as a teacher.

Many more "regionalist" composers studied at the Schola, far more than at the Conservatoire. It seems strange that sectional or quasi-nationalistic music developed mored under d'Indy's auspices than under those of Saint-Saëns. The reason is that under d'Indy social source was not a pedagogical issue. Consequently it was never subject to deflating isolation, reduction, or analysis. Early proponents of musical regionalism in France—Deodat de Sevarac of Provence, Albert Roussel of Tours, and Guy Roparts of Breton—were products of Schola; so were the Spanish composers Isaac Albeniz and Joachim Nin, the Basque composer Charles Bordes, and the Canadian Colin McPhee, who made extensive use of Balinese motifs. For all these composers the *Cours de Composition* gave great support in providing systematic treatment of musics beyond the ordinary literature and exposing the theretofore obscure traditions of, for example, Gregorian plain chant, and the music of Renaissance Spain and Elizabethan England. Countering the tyranny of the "silly" nineteenth century, which propped up a few traditions and held down many others, not only freed sectional impulses; it also underscored some aspects of Neoclassicism, as a counterforce to nineteenth-century Romanticism and as a product of the reemergence and reinterpretation of Beethoven and the eighteenth-century Classicists. D'Indy may not have liked much of the harmonically jarring Neoclassical music, but his conscience as a teacher overruled his aesthetic views.

Another national tradition beginning to emerge in the early twentieth century was an American one. Between 1910 and 1925 Harvey B. Gaul, Arthur Farwell, Richard Donovan, Isadore Freed, Quincy Porter, Robert Sanders, Daniel Gregory Mason, Alexander Steinert, and Max Wald studied at the Schola Cantorum. All particularly Farwell, Mason, and Porter, were interested in developing consciously American musical styles, usually through the use of indigenous American materials. At the Schola Cantorum they could do so without fear of derision. There they also received the very best in technical training, and their work was reviewed by members of the most elite music circles in France. Mason, a most enthusiastic supporter of d'Indy, paid tribute to his teacher's willingness to let the student choose whatever musical materials he found suitable. D'Indy, Mason said, was concerned with the ways a student used his materials; "far from resenting [this] impersonality, one felt enobled by it."[28] D'Indy, he added, "has the French knack of discounting enmity by understanding it, and even by ironically rallying it"[29] The use of the materials, not the materials themselves, was paramount. For it the student's materials were of true worth, they had to come from the student's heart, and "there is in art, truly nothing but the heart that can produce beauty."[30]

The Schola Cantorum presented an alternative to the more narrow Conservatoire, and it also contrasted with the nineteenth-century German conservatories where Americans had previously studied. High standards existed at all these institutions, but the historical orientation of the German schools and the Conservatoire leaned largely toward the nineteenth century, the time of German domination in Western music. Scholarly work on music before Bach was just beginning to develop, and its influence had not greatly penetrated older music schools. D'Indy saw to it that his Schola Cantorum was not so narrow.

If some Americans went to the Schola Cantorum, however, many more went to a new school, the American Conservatory at Fountainebleau. Walter Damrosch, conductor of the New York Symphony from 1903 to 1927, had been in France during the war; as president of an organization called American Friends of Musicians in France, he was collecting money to help financially destitute families of French musicians killed, missing, or incapacitated in the war. While in France Damrosch decided it would be a good idea to have Americans in military bands receive the best possible musical training. General Pershing, always sensitive to any way the American military did not measure up to the English and French, approved the idea, adding: "When peace is declared and our bands march up Fifth Avenue, I should like them to play so well that it will be another proof of the advantage of military training."[31] Damrosch had become familiar with most of France's major musicians and music organizations. So when the music school for the soldiers opened in Chaumont in October 1918, it was able to engage the services of such notables as Francis and Henri Casadesus, Charles Marie Widor, Albert Bruneau, and Nadia Boulanger. "The soldiers realized that they were receiving an education in

music equal to that of the foremost schools in France or America,"
recalled Damrosch. When the American troops were withdrawn in
June 1919 and the school closed, "I [wanted very much] to continue
these pleasant and important musical relations by founding a
summer school somewhere in France, preferably near Paris."[32]
The result was the Conservatoire Americain, which opened at
Fontainebleau in 1921.

The importance of the American Conservatory stemmed large-
ly from one teacher: Nadia Boulanger. Considering the number
and quality of her students, she can safely be called the most
important teacher of musical composition in this century. In the
twenties the following Americans studied with her: Marion Bauer,
Robert Russell Bennett, Marc Blitzstein, Harold Brown, Mark
Brunswick, Elliott Carter, Theodore Chanler, Aaron Copland,
Charles Cushing, Robert Delany, John Duke, Herbert Elwell,
Ross Lee Finney, Richard Hammond, Roy Harris, Frederick Hart,
Irwin Heilner, Mary Howe, Harrison Kerr, Clair Leonard, Norman
Lockwood, Quinto Maganini, Carl McKinley, Douglas Moore,
Walter Piston, Bernard Rogers, Harrington Shortall, Elie Sieg-
meister, Howard Swanson, Louise Talma, Virgil Thomson, and
Joseph Wagner. She helped these American students express their
musical culture and later did the same for composers from other
countries.

One aspect of her aid was her interest in previously neglected
music. Like d'Indy, she possessed an encyclopedic knowledge of
musical literature. As Aaron Copland recalled,

> Nadia Boulanger knew everything there was to know
> about music; she knew the oldest and the latest music,
> pre-Bach and post-Stravinsky, and knew it cold. All
> technical knowledge was at her fingertips. . . . She had
> a teacher's consuming need to know all music functions,
> and it was that kind of inquiring attitude that registered
> on the minds of her students."[33]

The field of music history was relatively undeveloped in 1920.
Phonograph records were in short supply and covered very little
musical literature. Orchestral repertoires were similarly narrow.
For a young composer in the 1920s, exposure to lesser known music
was not easy to procure. When it was presented in Boulanger's

rigorous manner, the effect was electrical. The students came to realize the existence of other musics than those they knew, but historical grounding had an additional effect. An English composer, for example, would be heartened to learn of the great music his country had produced in the sixteenth century. The obscurity of Elizabethan masters may have contributed to the torpid state of English music from 1700 to 1900. The revival of interest led by Ralph Vaughan Williams, Benjamin Britten, and Thomas Beecham coincided with the twentieth-century renaissance of English music. American composers, also, now could explore their musical past as Dvořák, Gilbert, and Farwell had done, at the very center of the art world with a teacher who enthusiastically predicted that American music would "take off."[34]

Another important facet of Boulanger's thorough historical knowledge was her concept of *grande ligne*. Essentially, *grande ligne* is a horizontal approach to a score, emphasizing melody and rhythm rather than harmony and instrumentation, the vertical elements. Since the midnineteenth century, Boulanger felt, conductors, musicians, and composers had been victimized "by exaggerated importance given to the bar line,"[35] and forgotten that it is essentially a guide for rehearsals but not for grouping musical ideas. By 1920 many composers were instinctively grouping musical ideas within measures. Using one of her favorite composers, the early seventeenth-century Italian Claudio Monteverdi, Boulanger traced the beginnings of monodic, horizontal writing and demonstrated that this approach had never died out but, with new possibilities emerging in instrumentation, texture, and harmony, had simply been obscured in the eighteenth and nineteenth centuries. Reassertion of *grande ligne* opened new vistas of interpretation to composers and conductors, provided creative avenues long neglected, and made explicable musical idioms of esoteric origins not tyrannized over by the bar line.

Other general products of inadequate historical grounding were the hypermodernist tendencies of some early twentieth-century composers. Witnessing the cavalier rejection of all past art by such groups as the dadaists, Boulanger commented: "If we part from us the works of the past, and deny ourselves the emotions they diffuse, we are in fact denying the possibility [of longevity] to contemporary art."[36] Conversely, she spoke with equal vigor against those who rejected all present art as decadent: "to stop dead so as only to

contemplate what has been is just as great a mistake."[37] Both
secessionist views were essentially nihilistic, a postwar fashion with
which she had no patience. "It is far better to confess," she wrote,
"that virtually nothing happens for which we are not ourselves . . .
directly responsible, and we should look for our part of the blame
in each event."[38] While cynical belief that the forces of the world
are unfathomable and uncontrollable may be psychologically
satisfying in the short run, the ultimate result will be "so much
bitterness and lost happiness."[39]

The cynical nihilism of her day, Boulanger saw, could lead
composers in two directions, neither of which she liked. One was
personalism. The American composer Charles Ives was an example.
Put off by a society that refused to take his music seriously, Ives
retreated into his own world, writing on his own. Boulanger felt
inexplicability would result from this approach, as Ives's work
indeed demonstrates. She did not know of Ives when he was
writing; very few did. But she later commented that he had more
flair than genius.[40] Boulanger had studied with Gabriel Fauré in the
1890s, during the shift in French music away from the Wagnerian
and Romantic traditions that had overwhelmed French music for
over thirty years. She was suspicious of the Wagnerian ideal of the
individual artist, attuned only to his imagination and will. A
totally independent artist tends to be obscure. If writing in such
isolation became the norm for the creative process, art would
suffer. It would lose ethical value and be anything the artist said
it was. A devout Catholic, Boulanger could not accept such a
separation of aesthetics and ethics.

The opposite of personalism was an equally mindless following
of fashion. Composers who follow fashion, and not the evolution
of compositional style, have no clear idea of what they are trying
to say. Their music lacks any personality, and is merely music by
formula. Nadia Boulanger saw serialism as an example. While she
understood the claim of Arnold Schoenberg, whom she respected,
that serialism was a logical extension of the technical innovations
of the late nineteenth century, she also felt that a lesser or more
impressionable artist than Schoenberg, Anton Webern, or Alban
Berg, could become too easily enamored of the system and follow
it mindlessly. In a teacher of young composers her opposition was
understandable, and it was no accident that few of her students,
particularly the Americans of the 1920s, became serialists. Like

personalists, fashion followers ignored history. Personalists ignored the ultimate unity between art and life; fashion followers lost all concern for their own identity in their art.

Probably Nadia Boulanger's favorite composer was Igor Stravinsky. His music had the technical excellence and complexity that satisfied her intellect, yet at the same time great depth of feeling. The music had a personal stamp, but it was never obscure. It was difficult because it was technically absorbing. Boulanger accepted Stravinsky's turn to serialism after 1950, for he was then secure in his knowledge of his role in musical development. Indeed Stravinsky, as shown by his disdain for the indulgent rubato of jazz, shared Boulanger's belief in individual responsibility for human order. They were personal friends, strikingly similar in their personal and professional fastidiousness regarding punctuality and appearance. Fastidiousness was more than a merely superficial component of Boulanger's personality; it was very much a part of her approach to teaching, and part of the approach to composition she demanded of her students. A case in point: Elliott Galkin, from 1976 to 1982 director of the Peabody Conservatory of Music and a Boulanger student in the late 1940s, recalled her asking him, upon inspecting one of his scores, why he did not draw his bar lines with a ruler. Galkin responded that he thought it of minor importance. Mademoiselle then walked into another room and returned with a new score of Stravinsky's in which all such details had been attended to with typically meticulous care. "A composer who does not draw bar lines with a ruler," she said, "is like a gentleman who neglects to shave in the morning, or who has a button missing from his coat." (Galkin confesses to having been guilty on both accounts himself that evening. He did not even know about the button, but Mademoiselle noticed it.)[41] Her point was clear: attention to detail, no matter how minute, is indicative of work in its broadest setting. Such concerns illustrate the care with which Mademoiselle taught, and expected students to know, fundamentals of theory, and they also illustrate the formal approach she imparted with regard to the writing of music.

She had little regard for bohemianism in life style or in art. It was similar to personalism, too indulgent. For this reason she cared little for the music of Serge Rachmaninoff, with so many notes and such extended self-indulgence of ideas. His ideas might be interesting, but the embellishment muddied the waters. On the other hand, she recognized the melodic genius of George Gershwin, while comprehending his technical inadequacies. When he applied to her for study she refused him, fearing, particularly in view of his age, which was twenty-nine—old for a composition student—that the technical grounding she would feel compelled to give him might damage his melodic gifts. Ultimately she felt the essentially creative elements in music—the horizontal elements, melody and rhythm—to be of greater importance than the more technical ones like texture, instrumentation, harmony, and development. "If you are a genius," she wrote, "who knows nothing, learns nothing and can write masterpieces, good, it is a mystery of God. And I believe in miracles."[42] An artist needed both intuition and intellect to create, but the intuition was more important.

But most of Boulanger's pupils were not miracles. They needed to be trained, rigorously. Students, she felt, should master the language of notation the way a writer mastered words, so that the use of the language was instinctive and one was free to develop ideas. She placed great emphasis on chord dissection and sight-singing. Mastery of sight-singing enabled a student to comprehend not only the sound expressed in a musical score but the inherent musical ideas. She was unequaled in her ability to take a piece, scored even for full orchestra, and on sight extrapolate its skeletal framework, thus separating essential from extraneous ideas. She would do this at the piano, giving the student an immediate realization of the piece's sound, as opposed to its mere appearance on paper. Virgil Thomson wrote:

> Suddenly [the student] sees that which has caused him pain, struggle, and much uncertainty unveiled before him, without malice or invidious comparisons, as a being to which he has given birth. Naturally he is grateful. His work has been taken seriously [and] has received the supreme compliment of having its existence admitted to be real.[43]

Her playing also gave the students a conception of their work in terms of performance potential, rather than mere cerebral impact. This perspective kept them away from the personalism that Boulanger viewed as decadent. If the work pleased the composer, that was not enough; art must communicate as well as express. A focus on performance potential further directed students from potentially overly intellectual modes of composition, like serialism. To her such cerebral music ignored the prime force in art—intuition.

Beyond the promotion of natural talents and the training of intellects, Nadia Boulanger provided an atmosphere which helped the individual composers discover their own gifts and sensibilities. Writing about her teacher, Gabriel Fauré, she revealed much about her own teaching:

> The atmosphere of his classroom . . . was one of sanity and freedom, quite exempt from dogmatism and that narrow spirit of sect and school we associate with even the best educational institutions. As a teacher, he seemed to have but one principle: to understand his pupils, to adapt himself to their individual personalities and help them find their own particular road to artistic self-realization. Distinguished musicians of opposing temperament and talents . . . lived in the shadow of his personality without ever feeling the slightest sense of constraint. It was he who understood them and not they who had to understand him.[44]

Students could not write pieces *for* Fauré or for Boulanger. It was fruitless to try to find what either would *like* to hear. Students could only write what was truly within themselves. With each student, Boulanger understood what that was and gently fostered it.

Beyond this, she allowed any collective dynamics among a group of students to take their course. Ross Lee Finney wrote that the mixing of ideas among Boulanger's students was as important as the interaction with her.[45] Since many Americans were interested in the development of a uniquely American music, their presence as a group at Fontainebleau or at her Paris salon helped underscore, clarify, and promote these interests. They maintained a discreet distance from the more famous intellectual circles of Gertrude Stein, James Joyce, and the Left Bank in general. Of Boulanger's students only Virgil Thomson could be considered clearly as belonging to these literary expatriates, and it took him several frustrating years to gain entree.

This slight isolation was generally helpful. It could have been an intoxicating experience for a young composer to be thrust into the intellectual world of Paris. As T. S. Eliot wrote, "the chief danger about Paris is that it is such a strong stimulant, and like most stimulants incites to rushing about and produces a pleasant illusion of great mental activity rather than the solid results of hard work."[46] George Antheil was one American composer so victimized. The self-proclaimed Bad Boy of Music enjoyed a pleasant illusion of being an avant-garde composer and being in touch with Paris's intellectual elite. But his music was superficial in its modernity and lacked any genuine sustaining content. He enjoyed the personal friendship of Paris notables but never collaborated with them artistically. Consequently, his fame was brief. This was not a career Boulanger wished for her students; it was not art but charlatanism, and thus decadence.

This is not to say that Boulanger wanted isolation for her students. She developed an intellectual salon of her own. In the twenties major musical figures of the day like Ravel, Stravinsky, Honegger, Milhaud, Poulenc, Auric, Roussel, and Koussevitsky, as well as writers like Paul Claudel and Paul Valéry were often present at her Wednesday afternoon teas and at summer gatherings at Fontainebleau. "In my own mind," wrote Aaron Copland, "she was a continuing link in that long tradition of the French intellectual woman in whose salon philosophy was expounded, . . . political history made, . . . musical aesthetics argued and the musical future engendered."[47]

For a generation of American composers, the Paris years were a type of university experience. Their intellects were probed, worked, and broadened. In a competitive atmosphere they associated with others in their field from all parts of the world and with people in different but, as they discovered, related disciplines. They rose, or floundered, in an atmosphere of freedom and ambivalence. The vogue of Neoclassicism compelled writing in a terse, lean language which starkly revealed their artistic worth, or dearth. Away from home they could see what had real meaning in their musical and cultural backgrounds. Finally, they were comrades, and among them leaders emerged who seemed best able to express what, in varying degrees, they all shared. Virgil Thomson and George Antheil became well known in the Parisian intellectual and social milieu. Roy Harris was the best of those who pursued goals he set for himself well before arriving in Paris. Aaron Copland, the most accomplished of his generation, developed from his personal roots and goals but also found himself greatly nourished and shaped by his Paris years.

NOTES

1. Gertrude Stein, *Paris France* (New York: Charles Scribner's Sons, 1940), pp. 17-19.

2. Janet Flanner, *An American in Paris* (New York: Simon and Schuster, 1940), p. 8.

3. Virgil Thomson, *Virgil Thomson* (New York: Alfred A. Knopf, 1966), p. 72.

4. Igor Stravinsky, *Autobiography* (New York: Simon and Schuster, 1936), p. 146.

5. Ibid., p. 142.

6. Ibid., p. 130.

7. Eric Walter White, *Stravinsky: The Composer and His Works* (Berkeley: University of California Press, 1969), pp. 61-63, 268-69.

8. Stravinsky, *Autobiography*, p. 153.

9. Autograph in the private collection of Jean Godebski, quoted in Arbie Orenstein, *Ravel, Man and Musician* (New York: Columbia University Press, 1975), pp. 76-77.

10. Virgil Thomson, "Maurice Ravel," *New York Herald Tribune*, November 30, 1947, Section V, p. 7.

11. Quoted in James Harding, *The Ox on the Roof* (London: McDonald and Co., 1972), p. 66.

12. Virgil Thomson, *American Music Since 1910*, p. 3.

13. Aaron Copland, *The New Music, 1900-1960*, revised and enlarged edition (New York: W. W. Norton and Co., 1968), p. 61.

14. Ibid.

15. Isaac Goldberg, *Tin Pan Alley* (New York: John Day, 1930), p. 266.

16. Quoted in William Austin, *Music in the Twentieth Century* (New York: W. W. Norton and Co., 1966), pp. 258-59.

17. Interview with Maurice Ravel in *Musical America* 48 (June 1928), p. 87.

18. Vincent d'Indy, *Cours de Composition Musicale* (Paris: Durand et Fils, 1912); Book 1 was written in 1897-1898, Book 2, Part 1, in 1899-1900; Book 2, Part 2 in 1901-1902; and Book 3 in 1903-1904.

19. Quoted in Norman Demuth, *Vincent d'Indy* (London: Rockliff Publishing Company, 1951), p. 21.

20. Camille Saint-Saëns, *Les Idées de M. Vincent d'Indy* (Paris, 1919),

passim. Rust's works had been modernized by his grandson Wilhelm (1822-1892).

21. D'Indy, *Cours de Composition,* Book 3, p. 286.

22. James Harding, *Saint-Saëns and His Circle* (London: Chapman and Hall, 1965), p. 153.

23. D'Indy, *Cours de Composition,* Book 1, Part 2, p. 411.

24. Arnold Schoenberg, "A Dangerous Game," from "On Artists and Collaboration, Symposium," *Modern Music* 22, no. 1 (November-December), p. 5.

25. Quoted in Harding, *Saint-Saëns and His Circle,* p. 153.

26. D'Indy, *Cours de Composition,* Book 1, p. 16.

27. London critic Basil Deane, quoted in Laurence Davies, *César Franck and His Circle* (London: Barrie and Jenkins, 1970), p. 413.

28. Daniel Gregory Mason, *Music in My Time and Other Reminiscences* New York: Macmillan Co., 1928), p. 228.

29. Mason, *The Dilemma of American Music,* p. 143.

30. Vincent d'Indy, *Revue Musicale,* February 15, 1913, quoted in Mason, *Contemporary Composers,* p. 175.

31. Walter Damrosch, *My Musical Life* (New York: Charles Scribner's Sons, 1926), pp. 248-49.

32. Ibid., p. 264.

33. Aaron Copland, *Copland on Music* (Garden City, N. Y.: Doubleday and Co., 1940), p. 87.

34. Thomson, *Virgil Thomson,* p. 54.

35. Nadia Boulanger, *Lectures on Modern Music,* delivered under the auspices of the Rice Institute Lectureship in Music, January 27, 28, and 29, 1925, *Rice Institute Pamphlets,* vol. 13, no. 2 (April 1926), p. 187.

36. Interview with Nadia Boulanger, quoted in Alan Kendall, *The Tender Tyrant: Nadia Boulanger, A Life Devoted to Music* (London: McDonald and Jane's, 1976), p. 112.

37. Ibid.

38. *Le Monde Musical,* January 15-30, 1920.

39. Ibid., May 1919.

40. Quoted by John Kirkpatrick in a letter to Alan Levy, October 6, 1976.

41. Elliott Galkin, interview with Alan Levy, July 12, 1976.

42. Quoted in Alan Kendall, *The Tender Tyrant,* p. 115.

43. Virgil Thomson, " 'Greatest Music Teacher'—at 75," *New York Times Magazine,* February 4, 1962, p. 33.

44. Boulanger, *Lectures on Modern Music,* p. 124.

45. Ross Lee Finney, letter to Alan Levy, April 13, 1976.

46. T. S. Eliot, letter to Robert McAlmon, May 22, 1921, in the Robert McAlmon papers, private collection of Norman Holmes Pearson.

47. Copland, *Copland on Music,* p. 86.

EXPATRIATES, FRIVOLOUS
AND SERIOUS:
GEORGE ANTHEIL
4 AND VIRGIL THOMSON

A common image of Paris in the 1920s is that of the Left Bank, that intellectual milieu with all its brilliance, decadence, innovation, tragedy; heated, wine-laden debates on aesthetics till 4:00 A.M.; a collection of geniuses and would-be geniuses, a world of an intensity never seen before and probably never again. The perspective of the 1930s, which naturally emphasizes the decadence of the "roaring twenties," remains very much intact as a popular view of this phenomenon. There comes to us thus a jolly, occasionally brilliant bunch of bohemians. But this image is simplistic. The sensitivity to the pitfalls of Paris's heady atmosphere shown by Eliot and Boulanger reveals that some important people of the time dealt totally seriously with art, an altogether different view from that a 1930s perspective implies. Two aspects of Parisian life, the brilliant flowering of the arts and the hard work, had great influence on Americans there. For some the two combined and the experience was productive. For others they conflicted and the result was maladjustment and frivolity. Two American musicians clearly at the center of Parisian intellectual life, Virgil Thomson and George Antheil, illustrate the contrast.

Though the best-known American composer in 1925 was probably Gershwin, Antheil was not far behind, and he was well ahead of others of his generation now more famous—Aaron Copland, Roy Harris, Roger Sessions, and Virgil Thomson. Copland and Thomson themselves said they had thought Antheil the leading figure of their generation.[1] By 1930 Antheil had all but disappeared from the world of music. His ephemeral career illustrates the danger T. S. Eliot and Nadia Boulanger saw in the Paris intellectual world.

At twenty-two, after a normal music conservatory background in New Jersey and Philadelphia, Antheil traveled to Europe as a concert pianist. This was not necessarily something expected. He saw the chance only four months before departure and seized it.

> I watched the musical trade papers. One day in middle February 1922 I saw that the well-known New York impresario Martin H. Hanson was going to Europe in late May. In another part of the journal it stated that the young pianist Leo Ornstein was leaving the concert management of M. H. Hanson. . . . Hanson had lost one of his main drawing cards and was going to Europe. . . . I practiced for one full month. . . . I played for Hanson [and] took him off his feet.[2]

Antheil always had an uncanny instinct for meeting, though sometimes superficially, the needs of a particular situation. The cagey instincts that got him to Europe continued to show themselves in his concert performances.

The premiere of Stravinsky's *Le Sacre du Printemps* in 1913 had caused a public riot. After that, such a reaction to modern music became almost commonplace and, in a perverse way, expected. A few hypermodern artists created works deliberately to shock. And some, claiming to be artists and wishing to show sympathy for an artistic modernity they often could not begin to uderstand, went to such concerts ready, hoping, verbally or physically, to defend the moderns against attack. Antheil wrote of one such affair:

> I commenced playing. Rioting broke out almost immediately. I remember Man Ray punching somebody in the nose in the front row. Marcel Duchamps was arguing with somebody else in the second row. In a box nearby Erik Satie was shouting, "What precision, what precision!" and applauding. . . . A big burly poet got into one of the boxes and yelled, "You are all pigs!" In the gallery the police came in and arrested the surrealists who, liking the music, were punching everybody who objected.[3]

Antheil had a holster sewn into his concert coat and would occasionally brandish a thirty-eight automatic if that evening he wanted his *scandale* to be a quiet one. Lost in this shuffle of performers, hypermodernists, and proper ladies and gentlemen was the sincere artist. Schoenberg, Stravinsky, and Picasso, for example, rarely attended such exhibitions and cared little for any *succès du scandale*. It was the lesser artist, the charlatan, who thrived on and exploited this aspect of the postwar art world. It was only an aspect, though, and a minor one, certainly not the whole picture as thirties commentators have sometimes suggested. Only this part of the twenties was noisy, highly publicized, and naughty. George Antheil rode the wave and when currents shifted quickly sank.

Antheil was naughty not only as a performer but as a composer. He had, if not a good ear, a good nose for public demand. Europe, particularly Paris, seemed fascinated with the primitive. Antheil, cultivating the look of a seventeen-year-old, provided trappings of innocence of things past which Parisians wanted to remember. He also catered to their interest in jazz and ragtime. As an American he was taken for someone who knew these idioms. To any depth he did not. Nevertheless, ever eager to be popular, Antheil wrote a Jazz Sonata (1925) for piano, a hodgepodge of jazz rhythms and melodies with little originality or integration of elements. Audiences took to it, particularly in the form Antheil skillfully chose to present it, as a concert encore, a frothy dessert served after a large meal when the palate is dulled and the mind fatigued.

Coupled with Parisians' interest in the primitive was a fascination with artistic renderings of modern mechanics on the part of futurists, dadaists and surrealists. Such "machine" art as works of George Scheeler and Marcel Duchamp appeared at this time, as did Arthur Honegger's musical locomotive *Pacific 231* (1924) and Serge Prokofiev's ballet *Le Pas d'acier* (1925-27). Antheil presented piano works like *Sonata Sauvage* (1922), *Mechanisms* (1922), and *Airplane Sonata* (1923), in which he mimed the clangorous, powerful aura of the newfangled machinery which had so caught the fancy of art consumers. As with the primitivism of the Jazz Sonata, the futurism here was superficial, music by recipe. To accommodate the mechanical trappings, Antheil mimed the musical style of his idol Igor Stravinsky. This was a good choice, as Stravinsky's rhythmic intensity and complexity complemented, and occasionally overwhelmed, the rhythms of jazz or machines. Antheil's version resulted in a glitter of vibrant, savage music which caught on, and Antheil became the rage. Ernest Hemingway expressed the only misgivings among the avant-garde when he soberly mused: "I preferred my Stravinsky straight."[4]

Antheil's most famous "mechanical" piece—*Ballet Mécanique* (1925)—marked the apex of his notoriety. It was originally scored for pianola, four xylophones, glockenspiel, gong, cymbal, woodblock, triangle, tambourine, military drum, tenor drum, bass drum, two electric doorbells, and two airplane motors (propellers optional). Antheil himself described its premiere at a Paris party in 1925:

> At the first chord the roof nearly lifted from the ceiling! A number of persons instantly fell over from the gigantic concussion. The remainder . . . squirmed like live sardines in a can; the pianos boomed mightily and in a strange synchronization.
>
> At the end of this most sweaty concert, champagne was served in great quantity, and the people were very thirsty, not to say shaken and distraught.
>
> I will not . . . claim that the elite of blueblood Paris imbibed more than was good for them, but I will say that they were all greatly shaken and needed refreshment, and that . . . was instantly at hand—a detail . . . I had not overlooked for this strategic moment.[5]

At the New York premiere in Carnegie Hall in 1927 Antheil recalled one old man waving a white handkerchief on his walking stick.[6] With *Ballet Mécanique* the various elements of Parisian sensibilities upon which Antheil had capitalized—the primitive, the mechanical, and the naughty—came together. And Antheil's superficiality also emerged. He said of his encore pieces for piano: "I invariably closed with a piece or two of my own . . . or something equally cacophonous."[7] Cacophony, not musical substance, was the thing. The relish with which he remembered the premiere of *Ballet Mécanique* shows his self-image as an *enfant-terrible*. His surprise at the "strange synchronization" is evidence that he cared little for the sound of the piece while writing it; his main concern was the right time to serve the champagne. Basically he wanted to create not music, but an event. Since Parisians wanted, needed, such events, he had a quick affair.

Not only as a pianist and composer but in his personal associations and life style Antheil fitted the moment. He took an apartment a floor above Sylvia Beach's bookstore, Shakespeare and Company, and associated with such notables as James Joyce, Robert McAlmon, Ezra Pound, Igor Stravinsky, Gertrude Stein, T. S. Eliot, Ernest Hemingway, Wyndham Lewis, Jean Cocteau, Ford Maddox Ford, Darius Milhaud, Erik Satie, Arthur Honegger, Nadia Boulanger, Vladimir Golschmann, and Virgil Thomson. Stravinsky expressed interest in some of Antheil's music, and Ezra Pound proclaimed Antheil a genius.[8] Like many artists of the era, Pound and Stravinsky were fascinated with America's musical potential and eager to snap up anything American, and Antheil was on the spot. He was a competent pianist, sympathetic to modern idioms, and with these modest "references" and the fact that few other American composers were yet known, Antheil scaled the intellectual tower of Paris, boosted by his youthful appearance, charm, and self-confessed "sheer brass."[9] He made his mark, but not for long.

For a composer to have lasting impact his music must touch the heart and stimulate the intellect. Antheil's did neither; it merely hit a nerve. He struck the momentary fancy of the Paris intellectual world but never touched its true depths. Pound's fascination with Antheil, for example, stemmed from his blind assertion that "if America has given or is to give anything to general aesthetics it is presumably an aesthetic of machinery or porcelain baths, of cubic rooms painted with Ripolin, hospital wards with patent dust-proof corners and ventilating appliances."[10] In the music that emerged in the twenties and thirties America contributed much to general aesthetics but hardly in the manner which Pound predicted. Defiantly modern in his art, Pound always strove to turn from past standards. Consequently he saw America in thoroughly modern terms, in greater contrast with Europe than was actually the case, and elevated the element of rhythm to the place of the essential matter of music. Hence he liked the music of Antheil and Stravinsky; the latter clearly brought rhythm to the forefront of musical esthetics, and the former began to isolate it. In the *Ballet Mécanique*, for example, the instrumentation, with the partial exception of the pianola and xylophone, revealed Antheil's virtual disregard for melodic elements and his singular focus on rhythm. Pound seized upon this preoccupation and from it developed a full musical aesthetic, divorced from all contours of melody, as stark as a "hospital ward." In doing so he elevated Antheil to the level of "genius."[11]

Several factors contributed to Pound's aesthetic notions. He was, according to Antheil, "fighting for a stale old moth-eaten cause, the cause of the cubist age, for what he [Pound] termed 'the cold, the icy, the non-romantic, the non-expressive.' "[12] This cause had already been won, and most artists had internalized its esthetic precepts. Among musicians it had been further modified, accommodating melody as well as rhythm, within the rubric of Neoclassicism. But Pound was a purist, a "Don Quixote standing there, shouting all over a battlefield from which the opposing armies had not only long ago gone home, but upon which even the monument to victory was decaying."[13] The narrowness of his views on music may have arisen from the fact that he was tone deaf.[14] Rhythm, of which he had the utmost command, completely dominated. Thus warped in sensibility, Pound could, with sincerity, distort and elevate a man like Antheil.

Given Pound's stature, Antheil's elevation held, for a time. Antheil later asserted that Pound "was never to have even the slightest idea of what I was really after in music."[15] He felt embarrassed by Pound's praise, he said, but needed the notoriety to penetrate the art salons of Paris.[16] This rationalization, however, is unfair to Pound. Antheil's willingness to be thrust to such heights reveals his lack of integrity; for him personal fame was first. And this lack of integrity betrays the superficiality of his musical compositions and of his success. He should have listened to Nadia Boulanger, with whom of course he did not study.

Antheil was willing to capitalize on any situation and succeeded until other American composers like Gershwin and Copland became better known. Then his notoriety evaporated. Another evidence of his shallowness is the fact that he never collaborated with any of the famous artists of the Left Bank. This is a giveaway, considering how much of their artistic activity was interdisciplinary. (In *Mr. Bloom and the Cyclops* he tried to write an opera based on Joyce's *Ulysses* but gave up the effort.) The Paris literati all seemed to enjoy Antheil and his music, but they went no farther. Socially Antheil was charming; artistically he was second rate. The thirties image of the twenties construes Antheil's activities to show the era's frivolity. But the case was just the opposite. Antheil did not reveal the superficiality of Paris; Paris revealed his. Beyond time-outs for cafes or visits at (or above) Shakespeare and Company, Paris artists took themselves and their work with deadly serious-ness. They weren't showoffs; they were creators.

In the remainder of his career as a composer, until his death in 1959, Antheil wrote music rather conservatively in comparison with that of any notable contemporary. As Virgil Thomson said, "for all his facility and ambition there was in him no power of growth. The 'bad boy of music' . . . merely grew up to be a good boy."[17] Aaron Copland recalled in 1936 that ten years earlier he had said Antheil had "the greatest gifts of any young American." He went on: "something always seemed to prevent [his] full fruition. Whether this is due to a lack of artistic integrity, or an unusual susceptibility to influences, or to a lack of conscious direction, is not clear."[18] Actually all three factors were involved. Many influences in Paris tugged at Antheil, and among them he faltered and chose the path which led to quick, short success and required little integrity. The journalist William L. Shirer, who attended the premiere of *Ballet Mécanique*, recalled:

> What happened to this brilliant young American compos-
> er? . . . Years later when I was home on leave and
> visiting briefly in California, someone showed me a
> syndicated column. . . . It was by-lined by George
> Antheil from Hollywood. It did not concern itself with
> music. It was, in fact, a junky column of advice for the
> lovelorn. Could it be the George Antheil of Paris days?
> I could not believe it.[19]

When the New York League of Composers revived the *Ballet Mécanique* in 1954 the piece aroused none of the jealous hostility for which Antheil hoped. It was simply accepted as a curio from a bygone age. Today we wonder how an artist could make a splash despite little talent or integrity. We wonder also how the few examples of charlatanism have come to be taken as representing the art of the time. For the heady atmosphere of Paris, which could intoxicate a lesser talent like Antheil, stimulated the serious workers.

Among American musicians, Virgil Thomson is the best example of a serious artist who thrived in Paris. "I lived in Paris," he says,

> because it reminded me of Kansas City [his home town].
> . . . Paris can present to anyone, . . . since it contains all possible elements, an image of his origins. In my case . . . not only was Paris to be my new home town, but all France, so little did I feel alien there, was to be like another Missouri—a cosmopolitan crossroads, frank and friendly and actually not far from the same geographic size.[20]

While sharing some of the aesthetic concerns of Antheil, Thomson, like many of his generation, was also interested in expressing his native musical heritage. As a musician Thomson knew he also needed to develop his technical acumen and his intellectual powers. After a stint in the army during the war, he attended Harvard, where he encountered cultivated antiprovincial cosmopolitanism and a music department with a decided bias toward French music. Both seemed very much at odds with Kansas City. The cosmopolitanism of Cambridge, Massachusetts, was so indeed, but the French bias ultimately brought him home. It exposed traditions quite amenable to the musical articulation of a culture like Kansas City's, home to Thomson, primitive and exotic to Parisians. Thus in France he found a tradition of highest stature in which Kansas City was respected. So when the Harvard Glee Club toured Europe in 1921, Thomson elected not to sail home with them but remained in Paris for a year, studying with Nadia Boulanger. Then he returned to the United States until 1925, going back to Paris after that and remaining there, with a few trips home, until World War II. In these years he was very much a part of the intellectual elite of Paris.

The symbiotic relationship Thomson expressed between Kansas City and Parisian sensibilities seems almost glib. This puckishness was a trademark of Thomson's, as a composer, writer, and music critic (for the New York *Herald Tribune,* 1940-1954), and because of it he seemed, like Antheil, part of the frivolity and decadence of the art of the twenties. But Thomson was a more imposing and intellectual figure than Antheil, and sweeping indictments do not stand up when they are carefully applied to him, or to most other major figures of the day.

Thomson's development as a composer in the twenties occurred along three lines: interaction with contemporaneous French music, cultivation of his Middle Western heritage, and relationship with the intellectual avant-garde of Paris in general and Gertrude Stein in particular. His work was often derided by critics who saw only one of the three strands and failed to see the broader setting in which they constantly intermingled. Attention to this general interrelationship of Thomson's interests reveals him as a composer and intellect of considerable substance, with concerns far from frivolous.

Thomson has been labeled the American counterpart to Erik Satie, a label that links him with the "naughties."[21] Satie's interests, at least in the later years of his composing, were to deflate the pretentions of art music audiences and break away from the grandiose styles of such contemporaries as Richard Strauss, Scriabin, Stravinsky (before 1918), and Debussy. Critics unfairly refused to take Satie seriously, and of course he did write a few deliberately perverse works like Antheil's. In addition to misinterpreting Satie, the critics linking Satie and Thomson demeaned Thomson as well. The composer Theodore Chanler, for example, charged Thomson with "ouija board production" which creates music with "the air of a piece of 'automatic writing.' "[22] "Automatic writing" has pejorative connotations, nonsensical and frivolous. But Thomson, as a Neoclassicist, desired to supersede the overly elaborate writing of the late Romantics and Impressionists, who strove to move mass audiences by impressive and heroic works. Thomson wanted to communicate with individuals, and his style thus leaned toward precision and economy of means, clarity, and apparent spontaneity of musical statement. His compositions seemed hastily written, directed only toward small, rarefied salons. The "haste" suggests frivolity; "small salons" seems elitist. But to dismiss as elitist music not explicitly directed to the masses is itself elitism; it prescribes certain musical forms and forbids others. To charge Thomson with frivolity distorts his role in a serious crusade for less grandiose musical form and less labored methods of creation. His music was not more frivolous than Strauss's or Mahler's; different, less ambitious in form, but no less serious. Puckish, off-hand remarks, the Kansas City subject matter of some of his music, the superficial aspects of some of his techniques, and his associations with the Left Bank, however, have suggested decadence.

Puckishness can easily invite charges of frivolity. With regard to the actual method of composition, Thomson once chortled: "How you get pregnant, God knows. But once you're pregnant, you know what to do."[23] John Cage says Thomson invented the opening measures of his String Quartet no. 2 while napping before dinner.[24] These accounts suggest irreverence, particularly if one holds that profound music must be created in a more painstaking, somber way, the manner in which Beethoven, for example, wrote. As Beethoven's work is undeniably a yardstick for any serious composer, his methods seem a possible model as well. Indeed, Thomson, as well as Satie and Les Six, was aware of Beethoven's methods as well as of those of the later Romantics. But as leaders in the movement against the excesses of Romanticism, which had removed spontaneity from music, they saw laborious means of production as part of the problem. Thomson by no means disregarded Beethoven, but he did not idolize him either. Since Thomson, Satie, and Les Six tried to create more spontaneous music, they felt more comfortable with methods that differed from those of their predecessors. Their writings were not superficial by comparison. They were different, but neither better nor worse.

Failure to understand the historical perspective of Thomson and the Neoclassicists, combined with superficial inspections of Thomson's writings, can result in misinterpretations. In some works he did employ texts that seem childlike or silly. In others he used musical fragments from genres allegedly inappropriate for a serious composer. An early work of the latter sort was his *Two Sentimental Tangos* (1923), where in addition to his use of a "plebian" dance hall motif, a tango, Thomson experimented freely with modern harmonies, created by setting melody at varying, tango-like tempi while keeping the accompaniment steady. Publishers Carl Fischer,

Inc., snorted "Rank!" and called him a "correspondence student."[25] From a traditionalist's standpoint the world of art music had two enemies—the moderns and the so-called lower genres. Here, as a Parisian Neoclassicist from Kansas City, Thomson exemplified both and paid the price. The charge of "correspondence student" further implied that Thomson did not know what he was doing technically.

An earlier work, Prelude for Piano (1921), had subjected him to similar charges. An important characteristic of the Prelude is the frequency of open fifth intervals, which creates a terribly barren effect, quite beautiful, as in Debussy's *La Cathédrale Engloutie*, but devoid of contrapuntal interest, making difficult subsequent development of expositional material. This point of criticism scholars have raised with justification against, for example, Mussorgski. But a knee-jerk reaction to such open intervals blindly assumes the existence of a development section. In the case of Thomson's Prelude, however, the brevity of the work rules out any thematic exposition with contrapuntal possibilities. It is true that the affinity Classical and Romantic composers had for development logically kept them from intervals like the open fifth, but breaking away from eighteenth- and nineteenth-century standards, Neoclassicists like Thomson abandoned older forms and toyed with devices formerly neglected. Consequently music of the Renaissance and earlier times rose in popularity, and Mussorgski emerged a protomodernist. Since composers like Thomson wrote music structurally different from their Romantic and Classical predecessors, they could effectively use different devices.

Other deceptively simple harmonies are also present in Thomson's accompaniment to songs of William Blake. Here again he had specific purposes in mind. Generally Blake wrote simply worded texts, and Thomson saw no need to muddy the waters with elaborate accompaniments. In fact, the simplicity of Blake's method of pronouncement was part of his message against the overly elaborate writing of such eighteenth-century thinkers as Swedenborg. As Thomson and his generation were part of a similar move against the bloated, self-indulgent music of the late nineteenth century, the poetry of Blake spoke pertinently to them. So for Thomson the simple path of Satie and Ravel seemed a good one to walk, particularly in the company of William Blake. When writing for the contemporary poet Georges Hugnet, on the other hand, Thomson freely, and capably, worked with more complicated harmony and melody. He wrote for each situation he met.

In some of the Hugnet songs, "A son Altesse la Princess Antoinette Murat" (the first of three poems from "Trois Poems de la Duchesse de Rohan") and "La Valse Gregorienne," Thomson made use of French folk songs, quite legitimately in view of the subject matter. It was similarly logical for him to employ American folk song when writing music on American subjects. But here he encountered difficulties, and his *Sonata da Chiesa* shocked Paris critics at its premiere in 1926.[26] Later even such sympathetic critics as Wilfred Mellers and John Cage spoke of the work as "prankishly perverse"[27] and "hilarious."[28] The work consisted of a chorale, tango, and fugue; the tango was the naughty bit, though there was raucousness throughout. Naughtiness was not Thomson's intention. He was attempting to depict a black church service he recalled from his native Kansas City, not with sensationalism or condescension but straightforwardly. Indeed, Thomson, as an American composer in Paris, genuinely hoped that Paris would get to know Kansas City and its culture.[29] Unfortunately, aspects of a Kansas City church service sat uneasily among Paris critics.

While Wilfred Mellers called the work "perverse," he did concede that the sonata lay outside the realm of "high" versus "low" culture.[30] Indeed, such a dichotomy was archaic to Thomson. As a composer he wrote for whomever cared to listen and with whatever materials best suited his ideas. Boulanger wrote to him: "It is not the kind of music I would write, but it is entirely successful. I have no criticism."[31] Her point was simply that Thomson said what he he wanted to say in a technically proficient way, and sociological nuance was a matter of choice for Thomson himself. This was the type of criticism the time needed. Artists' rebellion from societal norms had been fomented by unfair critics who judged modern works by past standards, injected their own sensibilities into the works of others, and maintained the past high/low art dichotomy. In the twenties Boulanger was one of the few critics not so myopic. She represented Paris at its objective best, and her criticism explains why the city was attractive to so many artists.

In *Variations and Fugues on a Sunday School Tune* (1927) Thomson presented another realistic account of the music he remembered from his Kansas City boyhood, complete with wrong notes and slightly shifting tonalities. John Cage described the work as "a series of miniature crimes impossible to commit because no God-fearing or even music-respecting church would permit the performance of these works."[32] But if one listens closely to a typical Sunday school, such music occurs constantly. Thomson was merely being realistic. Cage went on to describe the work as "an escape valve for that resentment toward Protestant church music that Thomson . . . felt."[33] "Resentment" may be too strong a word, but here Cage is closer to the mark. Thomson was trying to show Paris and the rest of the world his culture, part of which was the Protestant church. The "resentment" is apparent in Thomson's use of humor. He was illustrating the idea that Protestant church music lies dormant in past values but need not stay there. Church music was resting on its laurels, like the church in general, not attempting to adjust, theologically or esthetically, to the twentieth century. Less didactic, but similarly inspired, was *Symphony on a Hymn Tune* (1925), where, as in *Sonata da Chiesa,* Thomson drew upon a wide range of musical sources—Protestant hynn tunes like "How Firm a Foundation" and "Yes, Jesus Loves Me," popular tunes like "For He's a Jolly Good Fellow," modes from pre-Renaissance church music, fugatti, a march, a waltz, and cowboy tunes. He wasn't trying to be funny; he simply used what he needed for his musical purposes.

In Thomson's employment of musical resources with little concern for sociological incongruities and in his use of so-called wrong notes, he illustrates two important trends in twentieth-century music. The first, Neoclassicism, with a return to music as essentially notes, made sociological overtones irrelevant. These overtones could clash for the audience if the music combined in ways appealing to the composer. This is not to say that Thomson was not aware of the effect such writing would have. But it is rather egocentric to assume that such effects are an artist's primary concern simply because they seem salient.

The second trend, the use of "wrong" notes, perhaps most overt in Charles Ives, extended from critical and public reactions to experiments with harmony beyond the bounds of traditional diatonicism in the late nineteenth and early twentieth century. In the twenties composers continued to pursue these expansions of the tonal palette in spite of, in some cases because of, these reactions. As they did, they sought examples from other musical genres where such "different" harmony existed unashamedly—pre-Renaissance polyphony, various types of folk music, and musical performances from the so-called provinces. The last of these was a source for Thomson sought tonal beauty in music that seemed superficially Kansas City childhood was particularly important. Perhaps his simultaneous affinity for the poetry of William Blake reveals his sense of the worth of youth and innocence for artistic inspiration. Hints of this lie elsewhere in his music written in the twenties. His piano work *Ten Easy Pieces and a Coda* (1926), for example, subtitled "Baby Pieces," but hardly a child's finger exercise, contains references to "Chopsticks." Like his French contemporary and fellow Neoclassicist Maurice Ravel, whom he admired greatly, Thomson sought tonal beauty in music that seemed superficially childlike but upon inspection showed complexity and difficulty. In this regard Ravel was an important example for Thomson and his generation as they turned away from the styles of the late Romantics.

Thomson's interest in the "childlike" was a basis for his collaboration with Gertrude Stein. Unfortunately, this has also enhanced the "naughty" image of Thomson. One historian wrote that with Stein Thomson "wrote wildly experimental, often satirically debunking works as a protest against a [postwar] world that had had its day. The protest was that of a child."[34] In virtually the same breath he pointed to Thomson as part of the effort by musicians of the era to deflate "Europe's post-Wagnerian pretence and egomania."[35] The latter statement, reflective of the turn to Neoclassicism, is quite true but hardly identical with the former. It is only logical to counter one stuffy artistic tradition with opposite creations. But this does not place Thomson in a generation of disenchanted intellectuals. Critics still wedded to older aesthetic concepts likened this protest to that of a child breaking away from his parents. The metaphor seemed apt, for the character of new works like Thomson's, with their spontaneous melody, uncomplicated harmony, and rapid juxtaposition of incongruent resources, seemed childlike. But "childishness" is not quite precise. As an anti-Romantic, Thomson's return to more basic principles of composition heightened his interest in absolute music, lacking in programmatic or overt philosophical content. Another result was an ambivalence toward the nonmusical content of musical elements, allowing a combination of different resources, socially disparate (cowboy melodies and medieval modes) but contrapuntally compatible. Still tied to the notion that profound philosophical content makes greater music and unable to forget the nonmusical origins of the elements, critics have giggled at Thomson's music as delightfully childish and missed his point.

Thomson's return to a more fundamental mode of composition was similar to Gertrude Stein's innovations in literature. "The time of composition," she wrote, "is the time of composition."[36] The time of writing, then, was not a moment to reflect upon or analyze her subject matter or chosen object of art. The tendency toward introspective analysis in literature had been strong among nineteenth-century writers like Baudelaire, Poe, and Dostoevski, and in Stein's view, as well as in the opinion of contemporaries like Cocteau, d'Annunzio, and Hemingway, had gone too far. Thomson and his friends felt the same way about the musical excesses of the late Romantics. The literary scholar George Haines drew a parallel between Stein and Indian raga music:

> The music went on and on, like the babbling of a brook, always going on, always slightly, but ever so slightly, different, but mostly always the same. One waited almost nervously for a crescendo . . . but . . . in vain; and gradually, . . . as one gave up expecting, it was soothing music, . . . and then gradually as one listened more intently it was an intensely interesting, even a revealing music. There was no blare of horns, but it was none the less interesting. Stein's prose is like that.[37]

The interest in the twenties in such exotic art in Parisian intellectual circles makes this comparison apt. It ties nicely to musical developments in that such materials also fascinated musicians of the time, Ravel in particular. It held interest simply as something new, but more importantly, as it lacked elements like motivic development and "blaring horns," it provided an alternative example to the Straussian (over)emphasis on those very musical devices.

"No one thinks," wrote Stein, "that is, no one formulates until what is to be formulated has been made."[38] Here Stein expressed a view which fundamentally challenged nineteenth-century views of the artist. The Nietzschean conception of the artist was that of a sacred individual out of whose tortured struggles emerge profound revelations. Stein reversed this: one's revelations are the genesis of the creative process, not the product. Therefore one need not, should not strive for the philosophical in one's writing. It is there, or it is not. Thomson spoke similarly about composition: "Style, . . . you have it or you don't."[39] It will come through inevitably whenever one writes with integrity.

Since Stein rejected the idea of linkage between revelation and the process of formulation, she felt no duty to express her ideas in traditional patterns, which seemed ossified to her. As one critic wrote, she preferred to present "a character as an entity alive rather than . . . as an entity pinned to the wall like a butterfly."[40] Independent of formulas, Stein abandoned the norms of order—a beginning, middle, and end—and development. She felt free to focus on a subject, abandon it, return to it. Her free-flow approach was not restricted to subject matter; it included words themselves. She created a flow of sound, ignoring the meaning of words, concentrating only on their auditory effects. Virgil Thomson liked her prose: "He understood a great deal of Gertrude Stein's work, he used to dream at night there was something he did not understand, but on the whole he was very content with what he did understand."[41] Thomson felt that by setting Stein's prose to music he could "break, crack open, and solve for all time anything still wanting to be solved, which was almost everything, about English musical declamation."[42] Of all the great Western languages English had one of the weakest vocal traditions in art music. Thomson knew this and felt excited at the possibility of freeing his linguistic culture from its torpor. A preoccupation with meaning, he felt, handcuffed any musician employing the English language, who had to tie his music too tightly to meaning.* As music is basically sound, and words are both sound and meaning, Thomson felt a musician would do better, when employing a text, to focus more

---

*An example of this lies in opera. Audiences are often frustrated with English-language opera, as they cannot "get all the words," failing to realize that such pristine declamation is impossible, and not expected in Italian, French, Russian or even German opera.

on linguistic sound than on meaning. Thus Stein's literature excited him greatly.

> My theory was that if a text is set correctly for the sound of it, the meaning will take care of itself. And the Stein texts, for prosodizing in this way were manna. With meanings already abstracted, or absent, or so multiplied that choice among them was impossible, there was no temptation toward tonal illustration.[43]

The collaboration of these two Harvard people was fruitful, since their artistic approaches, as well as their egos, meshed.

In *Susie Asado* (1926) Thomson complemented the overtly inaccessible text with a similarly disquieting modern score. The texture is thin, the line more percussive than melodic. The tonality is vague at best, and the few hints of it are in the minor mode. As in the Prelude for Piano, Thomson builds tonic triads on open fifth intervals and ends the work on an interval the root of which is the dominant, itself the fifth of the tonic. Yet he also makes brief melodic references to "Casey Jones" and to Protestant hymnody. The use of "old-fashioned" music is more apparent in another Stein piece, *Preciosilla* (1928). Stein's text here was even more modern, and Thomson let it stand without modern augmentation. John Cage asserts that Thomson may have been embarrassed by the text.[44] Perhaps, but he may also have felt that such extreme modernism could do with the help of accessible accompaniment. Accordingly, there is a greater emphasis on melodic line, thicker texture, more harmonic development, and references to "Jingle Bells." In both *Susie Asado* and *Preciosilla* Thomson merged two strands which underlay his artistic development—the intellectual avant-garde and Kansas City.

In *Capital, Capitals,* written between *Susie Asado* and *Preciosilla,* Thomson took middle ground between underscoring a modern text and compensating for it. The traditional aspects of the score are the references to French and American melodies and Protestant hymns. The rest is modern. The melodic elements, triads, scales, and percussive sounds combine seemingly at random. Thomson did not do this to effect incongruity. Rather, he gave evidence of having accepted Stein's notion regarding formula in art. Whether some elements combined congruously and others less so was not the issue, for that concern would have to assume that certain combinations, certain formulas, constitute a proper style. And Thomson, as mentioned, believed that style emerges inexorably. The subject matter of *Capital, Capitals* underscores the logic of Thomson's seemingly random mixing of elements. Stein depicted a conversation among the four capital cities of Provence—Aix, Arles, Avignon, and Les Beau—in which the four engage in dialogues and monologues, never paying attention to one another, never building upon ideas, never reaching any conclusions, an accurate portrayal of the minidiplomacy of Provence. Thomson's music— four male voices and piano—babbles similarly, structurally like the Indian music George Haines likened to Stein's prose. Wilfred Mellers sees a possible climax upon the words "as they say in the way they can express in this way tenderness" at which time Thomson presents one of his Kansas City Protestant hymns.[45] As the passage is one of the more linguistically traditional parts of the text, Stein may indeed see tenderness as a good trait beneath the din of non sequiturs passing throughout Provence. The Protestant hymn underscores this for Stein and Thomson as it further recalls something of each's childhood.[46]

Throughout these years, 1926-1930, Thomson was writing a musical accompaniment to another Stein text that became their best-known collaboration—the opera *Four Saints in Three Acts.* Upon first hearing Thomson appears to have felt, as in *Preciosilla,* that the modernity of the text was best accommodated by harmonically traditional music. This "intelligibility" impressed many critics about Thomson's music at the opera's premiere in 1934.[47] Upon inspection and according to more perceptive critics, Thomson's music is not so tame. As in *Capital, Capitals,* Stein presents no dramatic climax here, and Thomson creates no musical one. There is a bit of the same babbling effect. Moreover, as John Cage asserts, the music defies analysis; one can only gather statistics.[48] Cage used this as evidence to push his view that "the materials of [traditional Western] music are becoming impoverished."[49] This is a convenient deduction for Cage. *Four Saints* illustrates to him that traditional forms like opera have little value, no dramatic impact in contemporary times, and yield little of intellectual value upon analysis.

> No attempt to grasp *Four Saints* will take hold of it.
> To enjoy it one must leap into the irrational world from
> which it sprang, the world in which the matter-of-fact
> and the irrational are one, where mirth and metaphysics
> marry to beget comedy.[50]

Ironically Cage, from his radical perspective, implied here the
same point raised by conservative reviewers—that the work is
irrational, indicative of decay of traditional value. Cage of course
liked the world of the irrational, while conservatives opposed the
marriage of mirth and metaphysics. Richard D. Skinner of *Commonweal*, for example, wrote that

> the breakdown in various practical affairs in our
> immediate times is no laughing matter. . . . Accurate
> parallel is afforded in the apparent breakdown in
> . . . the less utilitarian enterprises [like opera]. . . . Ger-
> trude Stein's name has been fighting words in the thick
> of all this. . . . [*Four Saints*] will no doubt seem an
> almost unendurable debacle [to any right-minded reader
> of *Commonweal*].[51]

Tying this "breakdown" to the supposedly naughty intellectuals
of Paris, the *Nation*'s reviewer wrote that

> the Stein-Thomson number had about it much of the
> alembication, the archness and mild effrontery that has
> regularly gone with the Parisian cosmopolitanism
> of our cultural expatriates, . . . overlaid with apolo-
> getic smirks of fashion.[52]

Similarly, W. J. Henderson of the *American Mercury*, trying to
reaffirm older ideals of opera, speculated that the work had to be
a burlesque on grand opera.[53] It could not be serious. Lawrence
Gilman of the *New York Herald Tribune* echoed this smugness,
calling Thomson "a creative artist with a nice sense of showman-
ship."[54]

Leaving aside the incipient criticism of *Four Saints* as a frivolous,
nonsensical burlesque, indicative of social decay, there remained
another charge against Thomson along more technical lines. The
Nation's Kenneth Burke spoke of Thomson's tendency "to delve

into the self-protective mannerisms of Satie, Milhaud, Casella, and Rieti,"[55] and the influential Olin Downes of the *New York Times* declared that Thomson "is not apparently a musician with very much resources of harmony or workmanship. . . . [*Four Saints*] may remind the listener of the kind of thing that old Satie and 'the Six' were doing . . . ten years ago. And that kind of thing . . . can quickly become tiresome."[56] These two were in effect criticizing Thomson for being old-fashioned. Satie and his friends had had their day in the twenties. By 1934 the music world, now apparently more sober, had seen the "self-protective" sterility of their approach to art and gone on to better things. This assumes that Satie, Les Six, Casella, Reiti, and Thomson had written similar music, which was hardly the case. The similarity between Satie and Thomson was that both felt obliged to poke fun at the over-inflated. But this is not to say that Thomson's music or his approach to music was sterile. It was the perspective of the thirties that supported such a negative view of twenties art. But Thomson, Satie, and most others of the decade were serious, at times funny. A few artists were even frivolous, as is the case at any time in history.

Enhancing the critics' inability to take *Four Saints* as other than frivolous was Thomson's use of an all-black cast. Stein was displeased at this but, with reluctance, gave Thomson a free hand in all matters of staging. A *Literary Digest* critic reported: "The singers are all Negroes. They do not know what the words mean and do not care. . . . The Negro has no intellectual barriers to break down; he is satisfied with the beauty of the words and does not worry about their meaning."[57] To the *Literary Digest* critic blacks were perfect singers for a childish Stein text where the words' meanings were unimportant. But is not this logic circular? Blacks are inferior, as Thomson must know; his choosing them as singers revealed the opera as essentially frivolous. Serious opera required serious, white artists. This critic's interpretation fell wide of the mark in regard to Thomson's actual views on the matter. Indeed, Thomson's thoughts on his singers were sincerely matter-of-fact, as well as perceptive about Afro-American religious history:

> I had chosen them purely for beauty of voice, clarity of enunciation, and fine carriage. . . .[58]

> They resisted not at all Stein's obscure language,
> adopted it for theirs, conversed in quotations from it.
> They . . . took on roles without self-consciousness,
> as if they were the saints they said they were. I often
> marveled at the miracle whereby slavery (and some
> cross-breeding) had turned them into Christians of an
> earlier stamp than ours, not analytical or self-pitying
> or romantic in the nineteenth-century sense, but robust,
> outgoing, and even in disaster sustained by inner joy.[59]

Today *Four Saints* is seen as serious opera, though by no means traditional. Stein was interested in creating a landscape in which, as in any landscape, all is stationary. In the opera there is physical, and musical, movement, but not to anywhere or for any purpose that can be analytically ascertained. To enhance this stark contrast between *Four Saints* and traditional opera, Thomson created a startlingly original stage presentation, using props and costumes of cellophane with very little color, mainly black, white, and gray. It was this desire to contrast the abstract *Four Saints* with the color and pageantry of traditional opera, and not silliness, which made sensible an all-black cast.

The casting marked another attempt by Thomson to merge Kansas City with avant-garde Paris. John Cage called the opera a joining of "the matter-of-fact and the irrational." Indeed, Thomson saw the vitality these two worlds gave one another. He saw it in himself. Just as Charles Ives felt Debussy needed to plant some corn, Thomson felt that Paris intellectuals needed a little taste of Kansas City, perhaps to protect them from falling for an Antheil. Meanwhile, he and his fellow American musicians and expatriates needed Paris; here they could pursue art for art's sake, and here they could grow.

NOTES

1. Thomson, *Virgil Thomson,* p. 82; and Copland, *Copland on Music,* p. 157.

2. George Antheil, *Bad Boy of Music* (Garden City: Doubleday, Doran, and Co., 1945), pp. 9-10.

3. Ibid., pp. 7-8.

4. *Transatlantic Review* 2, no. 3 (September 1924), p. 341. Hemingway commented on "the short period of Coventry that followed" in response to his remarks about Antheil. He felt he had run the risk of being "dropped from the party," revealing the extent to which Antheil had endeared himself in Paris. Hemingway, nevertheless, should have trusted his instincts.

5. Antheil, *Bad Boy of Music*, pp. 184-85.

6. Ibid., p. 195.

7. Ibid., p. 7.

8. Ezra Pound, *Antheil and the Treatise on Harmony* (Chicago: Pascal Covici, Publishers, 1927), p. 146.

9. Antheil, *Bad Boy of Music*, p. 9.

10. Pound, *Antheil and the Treatise on Harmony*, p. 61.

11. Ibid., passim.

12. Antheil, *Bad Boy of Music*, p. 120.

13. Ibid.

14. William Carlos Williams revealed this in his autobiography *(The Autobiography of Williams Carlos Williams,* [New York: New Directions Publishing Co., 1967], pp. 56-57): "Ezra Pound would come to my room and read me his poems. . . . It was a painful experience. For it was often impossible to hear the lines the way he read them. . . . His voice would trail off in the final lines of many of the lyrics until they were inaudible. . . . He could never learn to play the piano, . . . but he 'played'. . . . Everything, you might say, resulted except music. He took mastership at one leap; played Liszt, Chopin—or anyone else you could name—up and down the scales, coherently to his own mind, any old sequence. It was part of his confidence in himself. My sister-in-law was a concert pianist. Ez never liked her." Virgil Thomson wrote similarly of Pound's opera *Testament:* "The orchestra contained a *corne,* or animal's horn, five feet long, that could blow two notes only, a bass and a fifth above it. . . . The vocal line [was] minimally accompanied. . . . The music was not quite musician's music." (Virgil Thomson, *Virgil Thomson,* p. 83).

15. Antheil, *Bad Boy of Music*, p. 119.

16. Antheil claimed that the concert scene in Paris was corrupt, critical praise varying according to the amount of money one gave a critic. The salons were, then *"infinitely more important"* (emphasis his), and Antheil desperately needed to penetrate them (Antheil, *Bad Boy of Music,* pp. 118-19).

17. Thomson, *Virgil Thomson,* p. 82.

18. Copland, *Copland on Music,* p. 158.

19. William L. Shirer, *Twentieth-Century Journey, A Memoir of a Life and Times: The Start, 1904-1930* (New York: Simon and Schuster, 1976), p. 241.

20. Thomson, *Virgil Thomson*, p. 53.

21. Wilfred Mellers, *Music in a New Found Land* (New York: Hillstone, 1975), p. 206; Paul Rosenfeld, *An Hour with American Music* (Philadelphia: J. B. Lippincott, 1929), p. 98; Chase, *America's Music*, p. 531.

22. Theodore Chanler, "All American," *Modern Music* 10 (March-April 1933), p. 162.

23. Interview with Virgil Thomson by Garrey E. Clarke, quoted in Garrey E. Clarke, *Essays on American Music* (Westport, Conn.: Greenwood Press, 1977), p. 175.

24. Quoted in Kathleen Hoover and John Cage, *Virgil Thomson: His Life and Music* (New York: Thomas Yoseloff, 1959), p. 170.

25. Ibid., p. 249.

26. Thomson, *Virgil Thomson*, p. 79.

27. Mellers, *Music in a New Found Land*, p. 207.

28. Hoover and Cage, *Virgil Thomson*, p. 106.

29. Thomson, *Virgil Thomson*, p. 127.

30. Mellers, *Music in a New Found Land*, p. 207.

31. Quoted in Hoover and Cage, *Virgil Thomson*, p. 106.

32. Ibid., p. 142.

33. Ibid.

34. Mellers, *Music in a New Found Land*, p. 206.

35. Ibid.

36. Robert Phelps, *Yale Review* 45 (Summer 1956), p. 601.

37. George Haines, *Sewanee Review* 57 (Summer 1949), p. 413.

38. Gertrude Stein, *What Are Masterpieces?* (New York: Pitman Publishing Co., 1940), p. 21.

39. Interview with Virgil Thomson by Garrey E. Clarke, quoted in *Essays on American Music*, p. 176.

40. John Malcolm Brinner, *The Third Rose* (Boston: Little, Brown, 1959), p. 94.

41. Gertrude Stein, *The Autobiography of Alice B. Toklas* (New York: Harcourt, Brace and Co., 1933), p. 281.

42. Thomson, *Virgil Thomson*, p. 90.

43. Ibid.

44. Hoover and Cage, *Virgil Thomson*, p. 144.

45. Mellers, *Music in a New Found Land*, p. 208.

46. Thomson, *Virgil Thomson*, p. 127.

47. *Commonweal* 19 (February 23, 1934), p. 525; *Literary Digest*, February 3, 1934, p. 21; and *Theatre Arts Monthly* 18 (April 1934), p. 247.

48. Hoover and Cage, *Virgil Thomson*, p. 157.

49. Ibid.

50. Ibid.

51. *Commonweal* 19 (February 23, 1934), p. 525.

52. *Nation* 138 (February 28, 1934), p. 257.

53. *American Mercury* 32 (May 1934), p. 106.

54. *New York Herald Tribune,* February 21, 1934, section 5, p. 6.

55. *Nation* 138 (February 28, 1934), p. 257.

56. *New York Times,* February 18, 1934, section 6, p. 3.

57. *Literary Digest,* February 3, 1934, p. 21.

58. Virgil Thomson, "About *Four Saints,*" liner notes for RCA recording of *Four Saints in Three Acts* (LM-2756), 1964.

59. Thomson, *Virgil Thomson,* p. 239. Thomson was quite prescient in these views, as Lawrence W. Levine ("Slave Songs and Slave Consciousness," in Tamara K. Hareven, ed., *Anonymous Americans: Explorations in Nineteenth-Century Social History* [Prentice-Hall, 1971], pp. 99-126), Herbert Gutman (*The Black Family in Slavery and Freedom, 1750-1925* [New York: Random House, 1976], passim), and other historians of black America have recently developed these very notions.

ROY HARRIS AND
5 STRIDENT AMERICANISM

One problem of developing an American music, capturing "the world Whitman envisaged," as Aaron Copland put it, was for the individual composer to conceptualize and thus define his America. Since cultural heritages varied greatly among Americans, these conceptualizations differed, and the result was not the emergence of *an* American music, but of many. The "provinces" spawned a variety of music in these years. So too did many ethnic and vernacular composers in genres of American urban centers.* This outcome, logical by hindsight, disquieted some nationalists at the time.

When used as an adjective of culture, "provincial" has held pejorative connotations of being narrow and awkward. Some members of a provincial culture—farmers, laborers—can ignore or even enjoy such an image. But any artist who wishes to speak to many rather than to a few meets a problem. Music nationalists like Henry Gilbert and Arthur Farwell did. They went about their task with a sense of mission. Constantly confronted by imperious critics who loathed any commerce with "lower" vernacular traditions, including those from the "provinces," Gilbert, Farwell, and their associates came to view their work as a campaign against

*Provincial and vernacular are potentially overlapping categories, but they are not interchangeable. "Provincial" is a geographical separation which, in pre-1930 American art music, encompassed areas outside the nation's major music centers— New York, Boston, Philadelphia, Chicago, and Cincinnati. "Vernacular" is a distinction of genre, entailing cultures rooted in the nation's various ethnic, racial, and folk ways.

imperiousness. Though an important part of their effort to cultivate
vernacular traditions, this fight with critics should not have taken
too much of their attention. But it did. Elite Boston and New York
critics balked at this cultivation by even as great a figure as Antonín
Dvořák. Critics like Philip Hale, Louis Elson, and Henry T. Finck
could not be swayed from their belief in a permanent separation
between cultivated and vernacular music, and cosmopolitan and
provincial culture. Confrontation only reinforced their sensibilities.
With lines drawn, vernacularists and some composers from provincial areas felt more unity among themselves than actually existed in
their musics, and they concluded that if only they could win their
fight against the elitist critics, a single American music could
emerge.

Earlier composers had avoided any fight with cosmopolitan
Easterners. Paine, Parker, Chadwick, and, to a lesser extent,
MacDowell tied themselves to the culture of America's eastern
cities and denied, often explicitly, the worth of any sectional or
vernacular traditions as sources of artistic inspiration. Concurrently, during their heyday the partrons and performers of American music centers regarded the small towns and the countryside as
a wasteland.

At the turn of the century, with the rise in prominence of Gilbert
and Farwell and the unnoticed work of Charles Ives, the situation
began to change. More self-reliant composers could avail themselves of benefits formerly available only to their cosmopolitan
predecessors. For with better means of communication, an artist
in early twentieth-century Iowa could keep abreast of the latest
New York developments as easily as his Connecticut counterpart
had done a half-century before. Thus an early twentieth-century
artist could be close at once to the avant-garde and to his roots.

But cognizance of the latest developments in the field was still
quite different from living and working amidst them. First-hand
experience was essential, especially for a young artist intent on
making a mark. An additional complication was study. Like
artists in theater or painting, though to a lesser degree than those
in literature, an aspiring composer has to spend some time in
formal study. In the late nineteenth and early twentieth centuries
composers had to go to music school, and most music schools
were in the major cities. Rarely can musicians master the intricacies
of music theory on their own. Equally rarely do students fail to

absorb the culture of their locales. Thus composers from the provinces typically study in New York or Philadelphia and then slough off much of their vernacular or provincial heritages, as happened to Paine, Parker, and Chadwick. Early twentieth-century nationalists, however, reacted against their predecessors; Gilbert and Farwell, in addition to trying to develop a national music identity, feared cosmopolitan corruption and therefore did not pursue the same degree of technical training. Their music suffered. For any composer needs technique. Thus those who wished to articulate a provincial or vernacular heritage faced a dilemma. How could they learn the basics without being overly influenced by the biases probably present in their chosen place of study?

Paris offered a solution. At first glance this may seem odd, as in 1920 no city in the world was more cosmopolitan than Paris. Furthermore, spokesmen for Parisian culture had been notoriously antiprovincial since the seventeenth century. With the political centralization under Richelieu, Mazarin, and Louis XIV, the court drew nobles to Paris and Versailles, and with this migration, virtually all cultural life in France began to emanate from Paris. Outlying areas became politically and culturally submissive, and Parisians regarded the provinces as mere backwaters. The term *les moeurs de province*, literally meaning "provincial mores" connoted boredom and emptiness. These views permeated nine-teenth-century French literature, perhaps the most famous example being Flaubert's *Madame Bovary*. Up to 1870 Parisian officials simply ignored the countryside, "where many did not speak French or know (let alone use) the metric system, where *pistoles* and *écus* were better known than francs."[1] But between 1870 and 1914 Third Republic officials engaged in concerted efforts to change the countryside. Through conscription, new schools and roads, and the standardization of weights, measures, and currency, the provinces were "integrated into the modern world and the official culture—of Paris," to the destruction of provincial cultures.[2] The blithe, high-handed manner in which this official policy was carried out reveals how little feeling Parisians had for their prov-inces.

Perhaps because of the cosmopolitanism of Paris, Americans from the hinterlands felt on a par there with their colleagues from New York and Boston. Every non-Parisian was so oafish that the distinction between east and west of the Hudson was meaningless. New Yorkers in Paris could not be high-handed with Midwesterners. They could try, but they were out of their element; their elitism fell flat. Placed on an equal footing with Easterners, provincial Americans were heartened.

Numerous anticosmopolitan currents in French cultural life accented Paris's stimulating atmosphere. With Rousseau and numerous writers of the later Romantic era, Parisians had faced plentiful criticisms of urban cosmopolitanism as a rootless culture. Political critics called it the culture of a decadent bourgeoisie, out of touch with true popular feelings. The popularity of American jazz and other "primitive" music seemed to show that this criticism had had some effect on various elements of the music world, including French critics. Parisians may have felt their cosmopolitanism overdone. They could not compensate by going to their own provinces without violating their historical traditions; here they were still snobs. But cultures like those of West Africa and black America were so far removed from French traditions that turning to them would change normal patterns but violate no traditions. So while America's urban cultural leaders were both antiprovincial and antivernacular, Parisians, antiprovincial within their own land, were attracted to other vernacular traditions.

While an almost Freudian fascination with primitives lay beneath some of the activities of French artists, their actions also stemmed from more practical concerns. Much primitive art exposed new avenues of technique, of which artists in many fields took note. African people produced cultural artifacts that Parisians found stimulating. Provincials from the United States, or from anywhere else, could conclude that their cultures also had merit, to Parisians and even more to themselves. This objectivity was marked for Americans studying with Nadia Boulanger, on whom the elitism of American critics had no impact. With that opposition removed, gone also was a previously strong element of cohesion among American provincial and vernacular spokesmen. They produced much music in the twenties, but no single, binding element emerged. Gilbert and Farwell had not expected this. The struggle against the critics had overlaid many of the distinctions between the various provincial and vernacular traditions and had made distasteful many of the musical traditions of Europe. Eastern critics, who had imperiously treated provincials and vernacularists as a single entity, had also apotheosized certain Classical and Romantic musical traditions from Europe. Gilbert and Farwell, in effect, internalized that perspective, turned it upside down, and came to apotheosize American music as being free of all European influences. Roy Harris, a product of this gospel, was perhaps the most famous American composer of the twenties who was both a provincial and a vernacularist, and he showed the naiveté in which he and his fellows were steeped in the wake of the battles with Eastern critics concerning America's relations with European musical traditions.

Harris was born in Lincoln County, Oklahoma, in 1898, lived there five years, and spent the rest of his youth in the suburbs of Los Angeles. He worked as a farmer and truck driver and studied history, economics, and philosophy at the University of California-Berkeley. Upon graduation he turned to music. From 1923 to 1926 in Berkeley and Los Angeles he studied orchestration with Modest Altschuler, composition with Arthur Bliss, and harmony with Arthur Farwell. In 1926 he sailed for Paris. Funded by a Guggenheim Fellowship in 1927 and 1928, he remained there three years, studying with Nadia Boulanger. All his teachers in various ways were sensitive to the issue of national identity in music. Farwell promoted it. Boulanger accepted it objectively. Altschuler, who grew up amidst the efflorescence of musical nationalism in his native Moscow, continued to cherish it after emigrating to New York, where in 1903 he helped establish the Russian Symphony to propagate Russian music. Bliss, an English composer of considerable merit, was of the generation of consciously British composers, the most famous being Ralph Vaughan Williams and Benjamin Britten. Harris's "Americanist" predilections, doubtless already formed before his exposure to these teachers, were reinforced during his schooling.

Perhaps due to his background in history and philosophy, Harris wanted to express his sensibilities in words as well as in music. "Great music," he wrote, "has been produced only by staunch individuals who sank their roots deeply into the soil which they accepted as their own."[3] This point had been debated among musicians in the nineteenth and early twentieth centuries. MacDowell took the view that national identity had no place in music, as the characteristics of a given musical idiom could be duplicated by any careful composer. Harris believed a unique experience existed in any culture, and only the person who had the experience could express the culture in an art form like music. Harris saw that this had happened in other nations and felt it ought to do so in America.

But in the twenties most American composers still looked to Europe for standards and guidance. Among his generation Harris was the most sensitive to this subservience. America, he felt, was distinct:

> Our dignity is not pompous, nor are our profoundest feelings suppliant; our gaiety is not graceful nor our humor whimsical. Our dignity lies in direct driving force; our deeper feelings are stark and reticent; our gaiety is ribald and our humor ironic.[4]

Overtly Harris was speaking about the United States versus Europe. By implication he was speaking against those in the American music world who had taken on European airs and denied the worth of vernacular traditions. Thus his stand against European hegemony was a call for provincial and vernacular assertiveness. He elaborated:

> There are moods which young Americans are born and surrounded with, and from these moods come a unique valuation of beauty and a different feeling for rhythm, melody, and form. It is precisely this spontaneous native feeling for distinctly different musical values which makes the problem of the serious American composer so especially difficult. His moods are not warmed-over moods of eighteenth and nineteenth-century European society, nor is his musical material rearranged and retinted formulas of the standard classics which our students, teachers, and critics and our imported conductors and performers have been trained to think of as the only possible music.[5]

Particularly in rhythm, Harris felt one could find distinctively American traits. He contended that American rhythms were less symmetrical than those of Europeans.

European musicians are trained to think of rhythm in its largest common denominator, while we are born with a feeling for its smallest units. . . . Asymmetrical balancing of rhythmic phrases is in our blood; it is not in the European blood. Anyone who has heard the contrast between a European dance orchestra and an American dance orchestra . . . cannot have failed to notice how monotonous the European orchestra sounds. . . . When Ravel attempted to incorporate our rhythmic sense into [the second movement of] his violin sonata, it sounded studied; it was studied because he did not feel the rhythm in terms of musical phraseology.[6]

Europeans, in his view, see a meter such as four-four in three possible ways:

in quarter notes:

in eighths:

or in sixteenths:

Americans, on the other hand, will see these three possibilities in this fashion:[7]

quarters:

eighths:

sixteenths:

Such rhythmic effects do indeed permeate much of Harris's music. Perception of these patterns, coupled with Harris's own writings, strengthened the apparent Americanism in his music and led critics to seize upon Harris as true musical Americana. "Harris's melodies," wrote Paul Rosenfeld, perhaps the most influential American music critic of the twenties, have

a certain irregularity and looseness, . . . like the sight
of a body reeling from side to side, staggering a little
and yet never actually losing . . . balance. Cowboys
walk in that fashion, extremely awkwardly and extremely lithely; and so a personal piece as the scherzo
of Harris's sextet [String Sextet (1923)] brings to mind
nothing so much as the image of a little cowboy running
and reeling about on the instruments, toppling but
never falling.[8]

The British writer Mellers later extended this Western image:

Harris's primitivism seemed almost gauche. In a work
such as the early Piano Sonata [Opus 1 (1928)] the
composer . . . creates a sense of crude, pioneering
vitality. . . . The momentum remains undisciplined and
is—like the original westward migration itself—directed to no clearly foreseeable end.[9]

But such characterizations, though clever, are suspect. The images
are inaccurate. Wagon trains did not travel aimlessly. Rosenfeld
had probably seen cowboys only at movie theaters and not in
action.

These descriptions were perhaps no more strained than Harris's
pretense of being a musical provincial. He fancied himself a Sooner,
and he had, of course, been born in Oklahoma, but after five he
had lived near Los Angeles, in an environment, as New Yorker
Aaron Copland described it, not very different from that on Long
Island.[10] Harris may have been copying Benjamin Franklin; in the
twenties bumpkinism was as fashionable in Paris as it had been
in the 1780s. Moreover, he deceived himself. Of one of his most
famous pieces, an orchestral adaptation of the Civil War tune
"When Johnny Comes Marching Home" (1934), he wrote: "This
was one of my father's favorite tunes. He used to whistle it with
jaunty bravado as we went to work on the farm in the morning and
with sad pensiveness as we returned at dusk behind the slow weary
plodding of the horses."[11] At the time Harris was five. Could this
have been a true memory? Harris was not a prodigy. He did not
take up music seriously until he was twenty-two. The statement,

then, may reveal a bit of overzealousness in a man trying very hard to underscore the "Americanism" of his music.

In the twenties and thirties many American musicians seemed to be waiting for a distinctly American music to emerge, one they could hold up to the world as theirs. Some critics wanted to use Harris's professions of Americanism as a ready-made framework for listening and analyzing. Examining a work of art with a bias, one can usually find what one wishes. Paul Rosenfeld and Wilfred Mellers did; so did Henry T. Parker, music critic of the *Boston Evening Transcript* from 1905 to 1934. At the premiere of Harris's Symphony no. 1 (1934) Parker wrote: the symphony is "American . . . in a pervading directness, in a recurring and unaffected roughness of speech, . . . in broad design, full voice [and] a certain abruptness in the progress."[12] There may be some truth here, but Parker overstated the "American" content, oversimplified the nuances and complexities of American culture, and ignored other important components of Harris's music.

Harris's Piano Sonata and Concerto for Clarinet, Piano, and Strings, both written in Paris, contain many of the devices identified as American. The asymmetric rhythms are there. The melodic lines, irregular and unpredictable in contour, do seem to wander as aimlessly as the paths of wagon trains were popularly conceived to have done. The open chords that permeate the harmony can be construed to symbolize the open spaces of the Great Plains. There is some basis for calling Harris's music quintessentially American. But such analysis ignores other influences. The open chords, as in Virgil Thomson's Prelude for Piano, illustrate the influence of French composers, particularly Debussy, and of late nineteenth-century Russians like Mussorgski, a favorite example of Nadia Boulanger's. While for Virgil Thomson the difficulties in motivic development, usually present when one uses open chords, were few in the Prelude, as he was writing a short piece, they were a problem with which Harris had to contend in the more extended Piano Sonata. This, as much as the inspiration of the prairies, may account for the rough melodic flow of Harris's early music. Other factors also contributed. Rarely does any melodic section of his begin on the first beat of a measure or end on the last. This, then, is music not tyrannized over by the bar line, containing a sense of *grande ligne*, revealing Boulanger's influence as much as that of the open prairies.

Harris's unorthodox rhythms parallel devices Stravinsky used in *Les Noces* and *Le Sacre du Printemps*. The hearty dose of Stravinsky which Boulanger administered to her American students thus reveals itself in Harris's music, though Stravinsky's and Boulanger's influences were greater than Harris would care to admit. This is not to say that Stravinsky's example alone led Harris into some of his chosen devices, but that the similarity is too close for coincidence.

Some European examples, as well as technical inadequacies, then, were as important as the inspiration of the frontier on Harris. The technical problems may have been critical. Walter Piston, a contemporary of Harris and a professor of music at Harvard, wrote:

> The slightly uncouth awkwardness, the nervous rest-lessness, he [Harris] would undoubtedly consider defects rather than qualities. If these characteristics are due . . . to the lack of technic [*sic*], let us hope the man can in some way be prevented from acquiring a technic [*sic*] which might rob his musical language of some of its most valuable attributes.[13]

In the twenties some listeners recognized Harris's technical inadequacies; many saw his potential. His teacher—Boulanger—was certainly aware of both. It seems odd that Harris would emerge from Boulanger's salon with such inadequacies. Boulanger, however, may have dealt with Harris somewhat as she did with Gershwin, with whom she refused to work at all, fearing to damage his melodic gifts. She did give Harris (who, like Gershwin, had come to Boulanger at a later age than most students) some attention but less than she gave to other, younger star pupils, like Aaron Copland. She knew what she was doing. Less fragile than Gershwin's, Harris's musical imagination, she felt, could profit by some technical grounding but might not survive more refined levels of work imparted too quickly. Thus the roughness that Parker and Rosenfeld attached to Americanism stemmed from technical problems. Harris himself denied the value of his Paris years and asserted much formal study to be a waste.

> The teaching of definite rules about harmony, counter-point, and form, this academic emphasis on rules that

> have been culled from the most obvious formulas of
> obsolete styles is of course so much dead wood which
> must be burned out of young students' minds before
> they can have any intelligent understanding of the
> nature of American music.[14]

Paradoxically, the development of Harris's musical identity may
have been due to Boulanger's benign neglect. Refinement, she felt,
would come in time, not in Paris. And in 1940 Aaron Copland
proclaimed: "There is no doubt that by now Harris has largely
succeeded in smoothing out the angularities of his style—fortunately,
without robbing his music of its special tang.[15] Harris, as a matter
of great pride, did not fit into the Parisian social scene, yet his
development may stem from the intentions of his Paris teacher.
Like the wise parent of a prodigy, Boulanger knew how a talent
like Harris's was best nurtured. And as is usual in such relationships, the child is often oblivious, and at times scornful, of the
parent.

Illustrating Boulanger's further influence, Harris, like many of
her pupils, made little use of the twelve-tone methods of Arnold
Schoenberg. He developed themes that transcended traditional
diatonic norms, but through modes, not atonality. Harris's use
of modes expanded his tonal palette, but within the traditions of
Western music, in contrast with Schoenberg's approach, which
on the surface seemed revolutionary. Harris resurrected devices
that had lain dormant since the eighteenth century and blended
them with some technical innovations of the nineteenth century.
This was the effect teachers like Boulanger and d'Indy hoped the
imparting of the full gamut of the musical past would have. Again,
one cannot point to Boulanger as the determinant in Harris's
methods, but her influence seems present.

With regard to Harris's harmony, Walter Piston wrote:

> The French school represents its nearest counterpoint,
> realizing, however, that it has . . . become a mild sort
> of blasphemy to find [foreign] influences in the music
> of this most original figure.[16]

The model devices Harris employed elevated his harmony from
diatonic conventions, but not to the outwardly secessionist degree

of some of his contemporaries, like Schoenberg and Stravinsky. Similarly, Harris's harmonies with open intervals and touches of dissonance are not revolutionary or unique, but similar to those of late nineteenth-century French composers like César Franck, Gabriel Fauré, and Lili Boulanger. The asymmetrical contours of his melodic lines, which avoid definite cadence points, accentuate the elusive aura created by his harmonies. Harris might prefer to link this to the soul of an optimistic frontiersman, yearning for something different and better.[17] We have no evidence to contradict this, but these essentially horizontal devices are another link with the styles of Fauré and Franck and a further reflection of the influence of Nadia Boulanger's concept of *grande ligne.*

Harris's structural devices show further European ties. His favorite examples appear to have been the seventeenth-century German composers Heinrich Schütz and J. S. Bach. Their contrapuntal structures accommodate his horizontal writing and aid his pursuit of musical forms of linear nature. In his Piano Trio (1934), for example, Harris developed his thematic material out of a single interval; thus the piece flows horizontally from the original exposition. In the Piano Sonata he worked in the same way: the piece began with a single declaratory chord, repeated with rhythmic irregularity, and from these harmonic and rhythmic elements he wove much of the work. Development from such miniscule fragments can take many directions, for the options are virtually limitless. This provided the basis for the comparison of Harris's music to a wagon train.[18] But this was not a uniquely American form of writing. One can find it in many periods of music history, particularly in the late eighteenth century, with Haydn, Mozart, and Beethoven, examples to which many Parisians had been turning. This is not to say that Harris was unoriginal but that, like anyone, he employed devices that others in the trade had found useful. Harris seems to have felt uncomfortable with any similarities. To be "American," American music had for some reason to be free from foreign influences. This tenet underlay much of Sidney Finkelstein's and some of Andre Hodeir's later criticism of the Paris school and of the Americans who studied there. Their criticism of Harris and his generation constituted a perfect inversion of the views of established American critics. While the Boston Brahmins disdained any "lower" provincial or vernacular tradition, Finkelstein and Hodeir summarily rejected anything related, however vaguely, to the Classical or Romantic symphonic traditions the Eastern critics so apotheosized. Both sides ignored the complexities and subtleties of the genres they were examining, preferring to substitute essentially meaningless sneers of "vulgarity" or "elitism."

Criticism undoubtedly made Harris aware that he was writing in "European" forms while striving to be American. Both a provincial and a vernacularist, he was bound to be acutely sensitive to any charge of elitism, further explaining his occasionally implausible overextensions of Americanism. He also had the misfortune to become famous. "Gentlemen, a genius," wrote Arthur Farwell, "but keep your hats on"[19] (a reference to Schumann's reaction to a first hearing of Chopin: "Hats off, gentlemen, a genius.") At that point Harris was in the spotlight. The codicil Farwell attached to his accolade added pressure. Now under scrutiny, Harris's earlier bumpkin posturing caught up with him. Further, as he was held up as a leading "American" composer, he felt compelled to lead with words as well as music. So he wrote with affectionate nostalgia for an Oklahoma past he had never really experienced. The complexities of the culture would have been more apparent if his experience had been fuller, but his merely vicarious links with Oklahoma allowed him happily to substitute myth for reality. Living in the rapidly urbanizing Los Angeles area enhanced his romantic conceptions. His goal of trying to develop musical value from his experiences as a farmer and truck driver was not impossible. But as Virgil Thomson wrote: "Roy Harris oscillates between extreme intellectuality, for which he has little gift, and a banal, a borrowed emotionalism, which he cultivates out of a yearning for quick-and-easy success. At his best, however, he is moving and interesting."[20]

Harris was at his best when he simply wrote music and stopped trying to be an American. When he tried to assert his nationalism and negate European influences, he tripped over himself. When he presented his music without posturings it was good. While its rough, unintegrated nature may indicate his personality, limited technical acumen, or environment, it is the product of a keenly independent imagination, which Nadia Boulanger appreciated enough to leave alone, an imagination capable of creating pieces at once tied to, yet distinct from, European traditions.

Virtually every vernacular tradition, except those of native

Americans, has roots outside North America. In most cultural genres Americanism extends from a mixing of elements of various origins, some European, some not. Thus American music could never be free from European influences. But the Americanists' enemies, the Eastern critics, were thoroughly wedded to certain European symphonic traditions. The battle against them led to several confusions. One was that the provincial and vernacular traditions had greater similarity than was actually the case. Another was that anything related to elitist symphonic traditions should be avoided. Harris accepted these ideas. His inability to give them musical actualization illustrates not his shortcomings as a composer, but the basic illogic of the ideas themselves.

Other composers shared Harris's concern with asserting the cultural importance of provincial and vernacular America, Virgil Thomson among them. He felt that his native Kansas City had something to offer Paris and the world. With greater skill than Harris at writing about music, Thomson was more convincing and, significantly, less noisy in his assertion of the cultural value of his heritage. He was from Kansas City; he wrote music drawing upon musical elements of his heritage; the music was good. That was enough. He never wrote, in music or words, of a single American music and never felt ashamed of employing musical forms of European origin.

Other provincial composers tended toward Thomson's approach, though without Thomson's outward trappings of expatriate naughtiness. Howard Hanson of Wahoo, Nebraska, was one such composer. Hanson, of a Swedish family that had settled on the Plains, used American materials in many of his programmatic works simply as a matter of course. Like MacDowell, he felt that a given program can be used if it has musical value, its geographic origin being of little importance. In musical style Hanson illustrated some of his heritage. Unlike Harris he did not try to underscore the "American" character of his music by connecting his heritage and his music. He let the music speak for itself. The typical works by Hanson were his Symphony no. 1 *(Nordic)* and *North and West,* written in 1922 and 1923, respectively. With surging dynamics and tempi and an interplay of dramatic instrumental combinations, Hanson created a melancholy and solemnity similar to that of another composer of Northern European stock, Jan Sibelius. Some writers have made much of the similarity between Hanson and Sibelius.[21] One important difference, however, is a greater presence of open chords (fourths and fifths) in Hanson's music. Inferentially we may then have music of Scandinavian character with chordal devices, as in Harris, which reflect the austere openness of the Plains. Indeed, beyond that, Wilfred Mellers asserts that the combination of Hanson's use of the symphony in its nineteenth-century Romantic form and of his modern chordal devices illustrates his pioneer heritage: the Romantic concern on the Plains "with struggle and conflict: the assertion of will that is necessary to create a new world."[22] Hanson thus becomes a musical counterpart of O. E. Rölvaag. These characterizations can be neither proven nor denied; they remain speculations. On the assumption that circumstances affect behavior, Hanson's comfort with the late Romantic symphonic writing, a conservative style for his generation, may have stemmed from a conservative music education—with the traditional, German-oriented Percy Goetschius at the Institute of Musical Art in New York and at the American Academy in Rome. Rome was not the center of artistic and musical avant-gardism that Paris was, and there stylistic similarities with Sibelius could grow unchecked. Nadia Boulanger would probably have discouraged Hanson. Though she liked Sibelius's music, she once remarked: "Ah Sibelius, poor, poor Sibelius! A tragic case!"[23] revealing pity for an extraordinary talent directed toward the forms and styles of a bygone era. She did not envision such a place in music annals for her top pupils; she preferred them to be more up to date.

Further underscoring the contrast between Rome and Paris for Americans are the examples of Randall Thompson and Leo Sowerby. Like Hanson the two were old-fashioned in musical style. Sowerby's music follows many of the harmonic and intervallic devices, such as triads and ninth chords in parallel motion, of impressionists like Debussy and Loeffler. (Although impressionism was old hat by 1930, Sowerby was attacked for being too dissonant,[24] illustrating the continuing gap between critics and artists.) Sowerby also used the traditional forms and melodic and contrapuntal devices associated with Brahms. Thompson, too, was primarily a symphonist in the Brahmsian tradition. Like Hanson, the two spent their European years in Rome, not Paris, Sowerby from 1921 to 1924 and Thompson from 1922 to 1925. Regarding the emergence of an American music in the twenties, everyone from Henry T. Finck to Sidney Finkelstein agreed that it should take place in a modern musical style. Harris was far more modern in style and much more nationalistic than the Rome-trained Hanson, Sowerby, and Thompson. Here again, though he would prefer not to admit it, Harris owes a debt to his Paris experiences.

If Hanson's musical style—that of Sibelius with certain technical differences—was at all reflective of his Swedish-Nebraska heritage, his music reveals a problem with the concept of the American music that so many hoped would emerge in the twenties. For if being American meant displaying roots, which no one could deny, American music would then take the forms of many European as well as non-European traditions, with some technical differences. Harris might have difficulties in accepting this, but Hanson did not seem to. Aside from contrasts of personality, an important factor in the comparative lack of stridency in Hanson's Americanism was his compositional style. As a Romantic symphonist, Hanson worked in a style historically linked to expressions of nationalism. Harris, contrastingly more Neoclassical, faced critics who instinctively tied his style to aprogrammatic music. A modern style in part better accommodated his concern for national identity in music, for an older style would not speak well to future composers. But modernity blurred his national character, and Neoclassicism's outward, "absolute" appearances, like its trappings of elitism, muddied the waters for some listeners and further stimulated Harris's strident assertions of Americanism.

Most other American provincials were more like Hanson in their assertion of musical nationalism. Douglas Moore and Quincy Porter seem to have secured perspectives on the issue. In response to a question of how to write American music, Porter asserted:

> If the composer has been brought up in this country he will be influenced by his environment. . . . We should not necessarily expect echoes of jazz, negro, cowboy, southern or Indian folktunes. A real composer is not an arranger. . . . He must contribute music which is vital to himself and to others, music so well written that it will be successful in conveying his intentions.[25]

Douglas Moore felt the same:

> I feel very strongly that we are . . . overconscious today of the problems of idiom. . . . Too many of us worry about whether our music is properly a reflection of America, or suitably international, in order to please whatever faction. . . . It is idle, of course, to assume that we shall be unaffected by what European composers do. Certain tendencies of this age [Neoclassicism] which they advocate, such as condensation, simplification, and a greater objectification of music, will naturally appear in our work for the reason that this is 1931, and that these are universal tendencies. But if we happen to feel romantically inclined, if we like a good tune now and then, if we still have a childish love of atmosphere, is it not well for us to admit the fact and try to produce something we like ourselves?[26]

For both, the issue of conscious nationalism was one a composer should ignore. They felt a composer would trip over himself if he tried simultaneously to be both composer and commentator. They ignored the issue of nationalism, allowing their pieces to fall into whatever categories they might. In retrospect, Porter was primarily anationalistic, Moore a vernacularist. Regarding their less self-conscious approach to musical identity, in comparison with that of Harris, it is of note that both studied with Vincent d'Indy. From him they received constant emphasis of the notion that form is of minor importance, providing that the composer understands its historical and musical meaning and employs it with integrity and care. Also significant in contrast with Harris is that the two were from the East—not big-city boys, but basically provincial. Porter, an old-line New Englander and a descendant of Jonathan Edwards, came from New Haven, Connecticut; Moore from Cutchogue, New York. Their environments were more settled and secure than Harris's; their approach to music less strident.

Traditionally an individual like Moore would have been considered a provincial. He would have had difficulty winning acceptance in Boston circa 1890 as a serious composer, writing works like *The Pageant of P. T. Barnum* (1924), in which he employed numerous nineteenth-century dance hall tunes. In the twenties the label "provincial" remained but took on new meaning. For Parisians had shown appreciation of, even fascination with, backwater

American cultures. Unable to assert their cosmopolitanism over Paris, New Yorkers and Bostonians had to take note of Faulkner, of Bellows, as well as of Harris, Thomson, Moore, Porter, and Hanson. Flaubert had implanted among Parisians the inherent pettiness of France's *moeurs des provences.* But Parisians could appreciate the mores of a foreign provincial and the vestiges of a foreign vernacular tradition. Americans found a home here, a home where they felt comfortable and creative. Here, to the consternation of both snobbish critcs and provincial vernacularists, rather than one single indentity, the variety of American culture could emerge.

NOTES

1. Eugen Weber, *Peasants into Frenchmen: The Modernization of Rural France, 1870-1914* (London: Chatto and Windus, 1977), p. xii.

2. Ibid., pp. 492-93.

3. Roy Harris, "Problems of American Composers," in Henry Cowell, ed., *American Composers on American Music* (Stanford, Calif.: Stanford University Press, 1933), p. 165.

4. Ibid., p. 150.

5. Ibid., pp. 150-51.

6. Ibid., p. 152.

7. Ibid.

8. Rosenfeld, *An Hour with American Music*, pp. 118-19.

9. Wilfred Mellers, *Music in a New Found Land*, p. 71.

10. Aaron Copland, *The New Music, 1900-1960*, p. 119.

11. Roy Harris, from notes written for the work's original recording, RCA, 1935.

12. *Boston Evening Transcript*, January 27, 1934, p. 29.

13. Walter Piston, "American Composers, XI, Roy Harris," *Modern Music 9*, no. 2 (January-February 1934), p. 74.

14. Roy Harris, "Problems of American Composers," p. 162.

15. Copland, *The New Music*, p. 121. (The same statement exists in the original edition, printed in 1941).

16. Piston, "Roy Harris," p. 77.

17. Harris, "Problems of American Composers," p. 165.

18. Mellers, *Music in a New Found Land*, p. 71.

19. Arthur Farwell, "Roy Harris," *Musical Quarterly* 18, no. 1 (January 1932), p. 1.

20. Virgil Thomson, "Intellectual Content," *New York Herald Tribune*, April 20, 1947, section 5, p. 6.

21. John Tasker Howard, *Our American Music* (New York: Thomas Y. Crowell Co., 1931), p. 524; and Wilfred Mellers, *Music in a New Found Land*, p. 33.

22. Mellers, *Music in a New Found Land*, p. 33.

23. Quoted in Antheil, *Bad Boy of Music*, p. 150.

24. *Musical Courier* 99, no. 26 (December 26, 1931), p. 34.

25. Quincy Porter, "The Education of the American Composer," *Musicology* 1, no. 1 (Autumn 1945), pp. 32-33.

26. *New York Herald Tribune*, May 17, 1931, section 4, p. 4.

6 A NICE JEWISH BOY FROM BROOKLYN

Virtually all major American composers between 1870 and 1930 came from families who had lived in the United States for many generations. Quincy Porter's and Roger Sessions's American ancestries, for example, reach back to the seventeenth century. One group, however, was an exception—the East European Jews, from whose ranks came some of the most important American composers of the twenties and thirties, Aaron Copland, George Gershwin, Marc Blitzstein, Solomon Pimsleur, Elie Siegmeister, Harold Arlen, Jerome Kern, Irving Berlin, Isham Jones, and Arthur Schwartz being the most famous. The Jews were the only recent American immigrants from whose second generation came any composers of consequence. There were no great Irish- or Italian-American composers in the twenties; only Jews. While the East European Jews were similar to other late nineteenth- and early twentieth-century immigrant groups, they possessed numerous characteristics which were unique, and these help explain subsequent cultural patterns.

The primary difference between the Jews and other immigrant groups was that the Jews comprised an entire cross-section of their Old World society. While few members of the educated, affluent classses of Italy emigrated, for example, among the East European Jews all levels came over, from Talmudic scholars to skilled artisans to subsistence farmers. Also, this immigrant group was huge in numbers and concentrated in comparison with most others. With such quantity and social variety, it could form its own autonomous community without entering the greater society. The Jews lived in ghettos in East Europe and Russia under extreme repression. In the United States, freedom sparked a myriad of creative impulses. Large Jewish communities like New York City's could spawn a wide cross-section of professions. Earlier Jewish immigrants, mostly Germans, had lived with less cultural independence than the East Europeans of later years. For German Jews the synagogue, the family, and occasional festivals provided for most cultural needs. Beyond that they were obliged, and were usually able, to join in the cultural activities of the Christian community.[1] But the more culturally disparate East-Europeans, spurned by German Jews as well as by Christians, did not do so. Nourished by the rising Zionist movement, they came to prefer autonomy. The Chinese on the West Coast possibly excepted, New York's East European Jews remained apart from mainstream American society and culture more than any other large immigrant group. With sufficient size and spirit, with the transplanting of all Old World cultural levels, and with a zest for work and creativity that came with their new freedom, resources allowed them to be independent at least for a generation. They developed differently, in kind rather than degree, from other immigrant groups and from contemporary American society. They had their own economic institutions, their own political organizations (often well out of mainstream American politics), their own language, and their own newspapers, theatre, writers, and scholars.

This ghetto, however, was by no means a mere copy of Old World society. All its growths had crossed the ocean but, planted in different soil, reemerged in different forms. Talmudic scholars worked in sweatshops under former common laborers as foremen. Women could now take direct part in politics. And a number of new cultural institutions appeared. In 1902 Hutchins Hapgood wrote of a new art emerging in New York's Jewish ghetto—painting.

> The last few years have brought the earliest indications of what may develop into a characteristic ghetto art. In the course of their long civilization the Jews have never developed a national plastic art. Devoted to things of the spirit, in an important period of their history in conflict with the sensuous art of the Greeks,

they have never put into external forms the heart of
their life. There have been occasional painters and
sculptors among them, but these have worked in line with
the Gentiles, and have in no way contributed to a
typical or national art. With the slackening of the
Hebraic religion [and the general flux of culture in
new soil], . . . the beginning of a distinctive ghetto
art has already made its appearance in New York.[2]

Some of the early Jewish painters—Jacob Epstein, Bernard
Gussow, and Nathaniel Lowenberg—pointed out three important
characteristics of their art. First, it dealt with themes identifiable
in the lives of East European Jews in New York. Second, it marked
an embryonic stage in the development of a new tradition. Epstein
held that Jewish painters, with their admitted technical crudity,
would gain greater mastery over the technical aspects of their
craft.[3] They were thus similar to contemporaries in music, like
Henry Gilbert and Arthur Farwell, who pursued identifiably
American music and whose successors would possess greater
technical skill; they thus implied a judgment as to the relative
importance of inspiration and sensibility over technique. Third,
the art had a definite urban flavor. As Epstein wrote:

The country, much as I love it, is not stimulating.
Clouds and trees are not satisfying. It is only in the
ghetto, where there is human nature, that I have ideas
for sketches.
    There is no nature in the sweatshop, and yet it is
there and in the crowded street that my love and my
imagination call me. It is only the minds and souls
of my people that fill me with a desire to work.[4]

In contrast, the Yiddish theatre of these years dealt with subject
matter beyond the realm of everyday existence. Underscoring the
distinction between Jewish society and the rest of the country,
Jewish dramatic literature contrasted sharply with the social
realism of non-Jews such as Stephen Crane, Theodore Dreiser,
and Frank Norris. New York Jews did not desire a drama that

emphasized such subjects as the sweatshop. Yet here was Jewish painting, like that of Henri, Bellows, and Sloan, that drew upon the everyday for inspiration. The difference was that theatre was not new to Jewish culture. A dramatist had a heritage from which to draw; a painter had none. Pertinent subjects belonged to a Russian past too painful to paint or were in violation of religious law. (Hebraic tradition forbids images, such as those in paint, in the temple.)

The country had no influence. The writer Irving Howe underscored this personally when he recalled that in his youth in New York much of American cultural tradition had no impact on him. "Emerson," he recalled, "was nothing more than a mere country poet."[5] It was only later that Howe, and by implication others of his generation, comprehended the universal appeal of the New England transcendentalists and thus a great deal else of American culture. But this was not to occur until the 1930s; it was then that the American scholars recast their image of the Puritans and much else of American intellectual traditions, after a previous period of torpor and Menckenesque distortion.[6] Until then Howe and others of his faith were oriented to a culture independent of older American customs and often diametrically opposed to them. Radical Jewish leaders evolved doctrines from socialist political traditions that at best had previously been on the fringes of American politics. And Jewish painters gave expression to an urban environment traditionally viewed as the very antithesis of that which inspires the most sublime art. The culture was altogether unique.

While early twentieth-century Jewish culture was autonomous, numerous factors brought American and Jewish cultures together. A major force here was schooling. When the first generation of American-born Jews matured, the cultural gap narrowed. Radicals became Democrats. Yiddish gave way to English, though an English much influenced by Yiddish, and Reform grew over Orthodoxy. All this came with a generation of Jews who grew up in American schools, whose language and customs were not those of the ghetto, and whose schooling enabled Jews to succeed in the larger American society. But this training also signaled the demise of many old traditions. When Jacob Epstein called for Jewish artists to engross themselves in the technical mechanics of their craft, he in effect brought on the same transformation. Jewish painters of the twenties and thirties—Samuel Kalisch, Morris Kantor, Moses and Raphael Soyer—were indeed more proficient than Epstein, Gussow, and Lowenberg, but not so identifiably Jewish and urban.

Even less noticed than the rising Jewish painters were artists in a field also beyond the pale of traditional Jewish culture—secular composing. In 1908 in St. Petersburg, Russia, a Society for Jewish Folk Music began, the members of which collected and notated scores of Yiddish songs. They published and lectured about them, gave concerts and adapted some of the materials into larger compositions. Some of the society's members later emigrated to New York, like Simeon Bellison, who continued to lecture and concertize. Another Jewish immigrant, Planton Brounoff, also worked as a lecturer and concert leader, collecting and publishing Jewish folk songs and writing symphonies employing Hebraic material. In 1911 he founded the Poale Zion Singing Society, further to propagate Yiddish music. Other Jewish musicians and music lovers, like Henry Lefkowitch, Mrs. Jacob Sobel, Jacob Beimel, Leo Low, Jacob Posner, Max Helfman, Samuel Bugatch, Vladimir Heifetz, and Abraham Binder, continued this work. Some of their organizations still exist.[7]

Jewish music was certainly beginning to grow in early twentieth-century New York, but it was by no means at the center of Jewish culture. Aaron Copland recalled that the idea of becoming a composer was so alien that his family neither approved nor disapproved. They were just nonplussed. "I am filled with mild wonder each time I realize that a musician was born on that street [in Brooklyn]. Music was the last thing anyone would have connected with it. In fact, no one had ever connected music with my family or with my street."[8] Economically comfortable families like the Coplands arranged piano and violin lessons for their children, though Copland remembered having to insist most strenuously on piano lessons: "My parents were of the opinion that enough money had been invested in the musical training of the four older children with meager results and had no intention of squandering further funds on me."[9] Studying and playing music for fun and enrichment did not violate cultural norms. But in 1918 music, and composing even more, was altogether unheard of for a nice eighteen-year-old Jewish boy from Brooklyn.

Like painting, composing lay outside traditional cultural patterns.

But, a testimony to the social breadth of New York's Jewish community, in the twenties Jews began to enter this profession. If we take Copland, as an example, we see how the development of a first-generation Jewish-American composer reflects the gradual, at times tortuous, route toward acculturation. Formal education opened up new vistas and new problems, and pitfalls and detours occurred along the way. With George Gershwin, unbridled genius took its own course, independent of social issues. Marc Blitzstein was an example in music, drama, and the politics of resistance to pressures for acculturation; unhesitatingly he tied himself to the autonomous, ideologically pure, radical Jewish community of New York, the strength and longevity of which were greater than writers like Irving Howe have cared to imply.[10] But Copland, like many more New York Jews between 1920 and 1940, shifted.

Aaron Copland's best known music—*Billy the Kid, Rodeo, Lincoln Portrait, Fanfare for the Common Man,* and *Appalachian Spring*—speak to a wide breadth of American sensibilities. He is thus popularly conceived as an "American" composer writing for a national audience, not for merely a sectional one or for the avant-garde. These famous works, however, all appeared after 1935. His earlier music was different, more reflective of his Jewish, New York, and Paris experiences. Copland belonged to the generation that began to bridge the distinctions between the older Jewish and American cultures. His post-1935 music illustrated the direction in which he and many of his people, for better or worse, were headed. His earlier work, at different times Hebraic, Neoclassical, urban, avant-garde, ascetic, and popular, reveals an artist and a culture in transition.

At eighteen, when Copland decided to pursue a musical career, he immediately realized the need for technical training. His first teacher in music theory was Rubin Goldmark. A pupil of Antonín Dvořák at New York's National Conservatory, Goldmark was sympathetic to the notion of identity, ethnic or national, in composition, but he "discouraged . . . commerce with the moderns."[11] Like any young artist, Copland was interested in the latest developments in his field. Goldmark's discouragement did not dampen his interest; if anything it strengthened it, and Copland continued to study the works of Debussy, Ravel, and Scriabin. This interest in the moderns manifested itself in the style of his early compositions.

His first published score, written during his studies with Goldmark, was *The Cat and the Mouse* (1920). Like Roy Harris's opus 1 Piano Sonata, *The Cat and the Mouse* touches eclectically upon many musical styles. To create the effect of two chasing animals, Copland allowed different, contrasting musical fragments to flit in and out, and the result was enjoyable if not overly absorbing, an ideal work for a pianist's encore repertoire. The frequency of chromatic lines and dissonant harmonies revealed Copland's affinity for the moderns, and this led to clashes with Goldmark. To his credit, Goldmark did not reject the work out of hand; he simply said he was not able to judge it. This reaction strengthened Copland's feelings of camaraderie with the modern composers of Europe. Feeling in some ways part of the avant-garde, wishing to inspect the moderns more closely, and recognizing the need for further education, Copland went to France in the spring of 1921. Just as technical training, Jacob Epstein knew, would inevitably change the ethnicity of some Jewish painters, Copland's European experiences would also change and broaden him.

Copland had ventured "west of the Hudson" only twice in his twenty years, to go to summer camp. Now he was quick to see differences between New York City and other cultures. Sailing to Le Havre, Copland befriended an odd, aloof Frenchman—Marcel Duchamp. Since Copland knew little of Duchamp's fame, he neither patronized nor idolized him, which doubtless pleased Duchamp. To Duchamp Copland appeared shy, but the Frenchman quickly discovered that beneath this shyness lay a genuinely adroit and penetrating mind. Their compatibility showed Copland's ability to comprehend another culture, deal with it on its own terms, and grow by contact with it. This he would continue to do throughout his varied musical career.

From Duchamp Copland learned as much as he could about Paris. Contrary to Duchamp's advice, however, he went to Fontainebleau in the summer of 1921 to study at the new American Conservatory. Like most French artists, Duchamp was strictly Parisian in perspective and felt Fontainebleau would be a bore. To an extent he was right, as Copland's teacher at Fontainebleau, Paul Vidal, "turned out to be a French version of Rubin Goldmark, except that he was harder to understand because of the peculiar French *patois* that he talked."[12] But at Fontainebleau Copland met Nadia Boulanger, then a teacher of harmony. "I had never

before witnessed such enthusiasm and such clarity in teaching,"
Copland recalled. "I immediately suspected that I had found my
teacher."[13] He studied with her for three years.

Just as Copland was captivated by Boulanger, she, like Duchamp,
saw the talents beneath his unassuming exterior. With Gershwin
and Harris she recognized the dangers of too rigorous theoretical
training, but to Copland she felt it would be of use. There was no
danger of damaging his gifts; her training and his Paris experiences
would only broaden him. "It was a fortunate time to be studying
in France," Copland remembered.

> All the pent-up energies of the war years were unloosed.
> Paris was an international proving ground for all
> the newest tendencies in music. Much of the music
> that had been written during the dark years of the
> war was now being heard for the first time. Schoen-
> berg, Stravinsky, Bartók, Falla were all new names to
> me. . . . It was a rarely stimulating atmosphere in
> which to carry on one's studies.[14]

This environment did not overwhelm Copland, as it did George
Antheil. Significantly, Copland's memories are of the musical
atmosphere, Antheil's of the general intellectual milieu. Copland
was first and foremost a musician, who could enjoy the Left Bank
but not be led astray by it. In Paris Copland would remain Copland.

Copland's music between 1921 and 1933 fell into two overlapping stylistic and chronological categories: Neoclassical and
programmatic. The development and interrelationship of these
styles reveal the cultural shifts he made as a musician, and a Jew,
a New Yorker, and an American.

Neoclassicism emerged in Copland's first music written during
study with Boulanger. He quickly grasped the focus of the Parisian
music world and pursued the compositional style practiced by such
greats as Ravel, Honegger, Krenek, Villa-Lobos, and Stravinsky.
Stravinsky was the most important Neoclassical influence on
Americans in Paris, an influence accentuated by his close relations
with Boulanger. For Copland the ease with which he imbibed
Neoclassical styles during study with Boulanger stemmed, of
course, from the strength of his talent, but an additional factor

was the affinity his Russian-Jewish background gave to his interaction with the Russian Stravinsky and half-Russian Boulanger.
Copland came from an ethnic group uprooted from Russian only
a generation before. The Russian link in Paris may have provided
for the young Copland a subtle reestablishment of cultural ties.
For there he worked in close association with Boulanger, whose
matriarchy stemmed from Russian nobility, and there he met
Stravinsky, more recently uprooted from his Russia and embittered
by the post-1917 events that prevented his return. Copand, in
contrast, entered Paris with the *joie de vivre* of so many young
Americans after World War I. But in his memory lay the knowledge
of the hardships of his people in Imperial Russia. He encountered
Stravinsky, adversely affected by the fall of that regime which
had persecuted Copland's people. The situation marked a reestablishment of some latent cultural ties and a subtle cultural triumph
for Copland. Thus reinforced, he could easily draw upon the
Parisian Neoclassical style.

The first piece Copland wrote under Boulanger, and dedicated
to her, was Passacaglia for piano (1922); it differs starkly from
The Cat and the Mouse. The latter is playful and episodic; the
Passacaglia deadly earnest and more integrated thematically. The
texture of the Passacaglia is much thicker, indicative of the complexities of counterpoint Copland was learning with Boulanger.
Her influence is present in several other ways. The opening section,
a tense series of half-step progressions with ever-widening polarity
between right- and left-hand parts, creates a feeling of extended
suspension, an effect Nadia Boulanger liked, in view of her concept
of *grande ligne.* The harmonic clarity and thematic unity of
right- and left-hand parts recall some of the piano writing of
Gabriel Fauré, her teacher. Some striking similarities in thematic
exposition and chordal arpeggiation exist, for example, between
the Passacaglia and Fauré's Nocturne, opus 63. Copland's expressed
enthusiasm for Fauré underscores the French composer's influence
on him. In 1924 Copland worte an article for the *Musical Quarterly*
on Fauré in which he called him France's greatest living composer[15]
and asserted that in him, a modern composer could find at one and
the same time guidance for experiments currently in vogue and
links with past trends. Copland's emphasis on the anchoring
of modern innovation with earlier developments indicated the

attitude he was developing about the aesthetic issues of modern music. He was an experimenter but not a secessionist. He did not believe, unlike many contemporaries, that the past was a useless encumbrance. One's place in the flow of music history, he and Boulanger felt, must be explicitly understood if one's work is to have direction and lasting impact. He felt music could not stand still, but he could not forget the past. For an American concerned with giving musical expression to his culture in a modern language, such a progressive view was essential. This attitude manifested itself in Copland's music. The opening sixteen-measure section of the Passacaglia, for example, seems almost atonal. But tonality remains. Like Debussy in *Prelude à l'après-midi d'une faune*, Copland expanded the tonal palette from traditional diatonicism, developing new tonal colors, but he never destroyed basic tonal principles. This evolutionary rather than revolutionary view of composing predominated among composers in Paris, in contrast with the apparent view of Viennese contemporaries like Arnold Schoenberg, Anton Webern, and Alban Berg.

Another aspect of the twentieth-century Neoclassicism in which Copland was steeping himself entailed a resurrection of eighteenth-century musical forms. The Passacaglia was one example. Another was his Rondino for string quartet (1923). In its eighteenth-century form rondino was a miniature version of the traditional rondo, usually a dance movement in fast tempo containing a theme that recurs three times, interspersed with sections of exposition, development, and recapitulation. (In musical shorthand the notation would be R A R B R A' R.) In the twentieth century, however, the Neoclassicists tended to develop their musical structure more organically from their musical elements, the very opposite of the Classical masters' practices. Copland followed the organic approach in the Rondino. Also in keeping with Neoclassical custom, Copland toyed freely with tempi. Eighteenth-century composers usually kept their rondos in strict duple meter, since they were writing a dance. Copland and his contemporaries were less strict. In the Rondino, for example, Copland wrote in duple meter but in varied phrase groupings: instead of 4/4 or 8/8 he employed alternating measures 3/8 and 5/8. The Rondino and Passacaglia both exemplify the strength of Parisian Neoclassical influence on Copland, the eagerness with which he pursued it, and the skill he had in using it.

Copland's use of a form like the passacaglia, one of the most complex and difficult of all eighteenth-century forms, illustrates the talent Boulanger saw. A student of his quality, she realized, could proceed directly to the higher levels of composition. He could absorb the technical complexities and master them without letting them master him. His musical personality, unlike Gershwin's or Harris's, would endure, indeed grow stronger, while he quickly learned formal techniques. A good illustration of Boulanger's perception follows:

> Mlle. Boulanger asked me to write an organ concerto for her first American tour, knowing full well that I had only a nodding acquaintance with the king of instruments and that I had never heard a note of my own orchestration. "Do you really think I can do it?" I asked hopefully. "*Mais oui*" was the firm reply—and so I did.[16]

The Organ Symphony revealed more fully than previous work the influences of the Paris music world, in which Copland had now been living three years. The modalic lines of the opening movement and the contrapuntal interplay between instruments of translucent color, such as flute, harp, and organ, exemplify the influence of the late music of Debussy and Ravel. But the patterns of Copland's thematic expositions are not so free-flowing as those of the Impressionists, illustrating Copland's stronger adherence to the employed Classical form, a major distinction between the Parisian Neoclassicists and their Impressionist predecessors. The Neoclassical influence is apparent in the remaining movements, where Stravinsky's example is important.

Copland's stated goal at this time was to express his many-faceted experiences. But he also knew it was necessary to acquire technical acumen. Boulanger believed both were possible. Effusive, full-orchestra passages from the Organ Symphony, however, reveal potential conflict between technique and sensibility, since they seem largely a product of technique. Copland's subsequent work reveals that Boulanger was right, but for a time Copland failed to achieve harmony between sensibility and technique. Ultimately a resolution came, and as Copland approached it he tried to sort out the various elements of his musical and cultural character. Thus variously he gave musical expression to his Russian-Jewish heritage, to his New York environment, to the Neoclassicism he had imbibed in Paris, and to the more general American culture as he then saw it. The emergence of each element marked a milestone in Copland's development as a composer in his relation with his culture.

After the Organ Symphony Copland wrote *Grogh* (1925), a series of dances scored for orchestra. Here various elements appear with little integration to show their relationship in Copland's mind. The starkness of thematic juxtaposition in *Grogh* diminishes a bit in *Music for the Theatre* (1925), the Piano Concerto (1926), and a blues piece for piano (1926), published in 1949 with three others as *Four Piano Blues.* All three works reveal a plethora of influences. The use of polyrhythms (various parts playing simultaneously at different meters) shows Stravinsky's continuing impact. The variation structure, also present in the Organ Symphony and at work in various ways in all these works, was a form which Boulanger taught extensively. Jewish themes, apparent in *Grogh,* are less overt in *Music for the Theatre,* the Piano Concerto, and the blues piece, where the center of the stage is held by another element of Copland's culture—America jazz and blues. Copland was here less Hebraic and more generally American. He had gained some notoriety by 1925 and 1926 and perhaps felt more confident in speaking for and to a wider audience.

The emergence of an identifiably American music was expected by many critics and musicians in the twenties. As his fame grew, Copland, who had returned to the United States in 1925, increasingly appeared as the leader of this movement. It might come about through a merging of two traditions formerly divided, art music and vernacular music. The most visible vernacular traditions in the twenties were jazz and blues. Thus, joining them with some complex forms of composition would seem a logical shaping of an American music which would at once stimulate listeners' intellects and excite their spirits. This is what Copland attempted. The blues piece contains the jarring syncopation, arpeggiated melodic rubati, and tonally unsettling ending—A and A natural—associated with blues, all within classical forms. The *Music for the Theatre* Copland cast as an orchestral suite, and the Piano Concerto in traditional three-movement form. Maurice Ravel and Igor Stravinsky had used jazz in some of their music, but merely out of curiosity about the unfamiliar. Copland did better. His use was not so episodic. He knew jazz; he treated it not out of sensationalism or exoticism, but as a musical source that was part of his culture, and here it was an integral part of his musical structure. In the Piano Concerto, for example, the polyrhythmic jazz sections are not used for mere decoration; they provide a base for subsequent thematic and rhythmic development. In *Music for the Theatre* another element exists. Early in the first movement Copland presented a theme the conjunct progression and slightly chromatic line and harmony of which suggest Hebraic chant. Subsequently a jazz theme appears. These two themes seem dissimilar, musically and socially. But Copland subsequently united them. When he did, Copland was implying from his New York perspective that the social origins of the two are not so disparate. One can hear examples of both in close proximity in New York; if they can coexist geographically, they can meld in the same musical score. Indeed, in the institution of the theatre such a merger had already occurred, so *Music for the Theatre* deserves its name. The theatre had previously been the stronghold of traditional culture for the East European Jews in New York. By 1925 this was beginning to change. Traditional Yiddish theatre had begun to give to and take from other theatrical traditions in New York,[17] and a similar confluence of Jewish and American elements was taking place in Copland's musical style.

Jewish and American elements were merging with the Neoclassical style Copland had learned in Paris. The influence of Stravinsky's percussiveness and rhythmic complexity appears in *Music for the Theatre* and in the Piano Concerto, as in the somewhat disjointed *Grogh*,* but it is more controlled in the later works. Copland revised *Grogh* in 1929 in Dance Symphony, which further demonstrates the composer's maturation. The various American,

*No value judgment is implied here. The disjointedness reflects the maturity of the composer's character, not the quality of the music. Indeed, as the critic Paul Rosenfeld wrote in 1929, "[The] musicianship of Copland's is still in its nubile stage. His gift is . . . as yet so immature that it makes the impression not so much of something human, as of something colt-like: all legs, head, and frisking hide; cantering past on long uncertain stilts, the body oddly small in proportion to the motorpower, the head huge and as wooden and devilish as that of a rocking horse. It's an amusing affair, . . . charming with the awkwardness of the large young thing not long from the mother."[18]

Jewish, and Neoclassical influences are present, but under far greater control.

Copland's simultaneous use of Jewish and jazz themes in the mid twenties demonstrated the logic of their integration. That he used "vernacular" themes in a symphonic medium illustrated his view and that of many contemporary composers of the poverty inherent in the traditional separation of art and vernacular music in American musical institutions. Cleverly Copland underscored this point in *Music for the Theatre* by using the theatre, an institution where neither the stuffy imperiousness of the art music world nor the lickspittle anti-elite elitism of the vernacular dominated. Since he was writing for symphony orchestra, he met much stuffiness from critics. Serge Koussevitsky premiered the Piano Concerto with the Boston Symphony on January 28, 1927, with Copland as soloist. Boston's tradition-bound critics panned the performance. The venerable Philip Hale, who a quarter century before had tried to minimize the vernacular-American content of Dvořák's music, snorted: "Copland's *Piano Concerto* shows a shocking lack of taste, of proportion. After thunderous, blaring measures . . . there are gentle purposeless measures for the piano, which is struck by fingers apparently at random, as a child announces itself by making noises when it is restless."[19] For years Hale and other critics had been engaged in verbal combat with modern composers, likening experiments and new ideas to the aberrations of misguided youth. Rather than contributing to musical understanding, these interpretations served largely to soothe the apprehensions of those who either could not or did not want to understand new developments. Henry T. Parker of the *Evening Transcript* had some sense of this when he wrote:

> Mr. Copland for aught anyone can affirm, may be the merest freak for a composer of eminence in embryo. A serene and distant future, not a clamoring present, will give judgment. Meanwhile, he speaks for a "chapel" of young American composers, for a new and experimental sort of music. . . . Not prejudice, but perception will reduce Mr. Copland to his level.[20]

Though disclaiming prejudice, Parker did not avoid the trap, though in reference to a time of history rather than to a group of artists. "Perception" is well chosen; "reduce" is not.

The conductor and musicologist Nicolas Slonimsky collected these and other reviews and sent them to Copland, who responded:

> You're a darling to have sent all those delightful write-ups. After reading them I went to the mirror to see if I could recognize myself. . . . Only one thing got my nanny: how dare H. T. Parker talk of *reducing* me to my level, while I am waiting to be *raised* to my level?[21]

There were some sympathetic critics, like Lawrence Gilman of the *New York Herald Tribune* and freelancer Paul Rosenfeld, but very few. Of musical criticism Copland wrote:

> People often talk as if they imagine it is the duty of the critic to remain severely aloof in order to guarantee a balanced judgment. But that is not my idea. A critic, it must be said, is not just a detached bystander whose job may be considered final when he has given the composer a casual hearing. No, a critic is just as much a member of our musical civilization as any composer is. . . . [As long as] they exist on the outer fringe, . . . [they will remain] a shortsighted lot.[22]

Shortsightedness led critics to develop a cataloguer mentality. They pigeonholed a composer, or piece of music, into a preconceived category and thereafter dealt with the composer or piece on that basis, a practice which misinforms the reader and debilitates the artist. Change in the composer's work goes unnoticed, and the categories themselves are often too rigid to accommodate the many nuances of a great composer's music. This is particularly true of the modern composers, who have crossed many of the lines demarcating traditional genres and styles.

Though the young American composers of the twenties wanted to break down the barriers between modern art and their audiences, in general they failed. Their works often met with snorts from critics and hisses from audiences. Conductors, who must face financial problems, knew they could not feed their audiences exclusively with modern music but must placate their patrons. At the premiere of the Organ Symphony the conductor, Walter Damrosch, a sympathetic modernist, "fearing that the elderly ladies in his audience have been shocked by the asperities of the new style in music [consoled them by proclaiming:] 'If a young man at the age of twenty-three can write a symphony like that, in five years he will be ready to commit murder.' "²³ This prophecy might do little harm, but limiting the amount of modern music performed did much. Except for Damrosch of the New York Symphony, who retired in 1927, Koussevitsky of the Boston Symphony, and to a lesser extent Leopold Stokowski in Philadelphia, American symphony orchestra conductors played little modern American music, Arturo Toscanini being a most notorious example. To meet this situation, in 1927 Copland and his fellow composer Roger Sessions began a series of concerts to make modern music available to anyone who cared to listen. Such a forum put the moderns in a ghetto, but the only alternative was neglect. The critic Minna Lederman founded a journal, *Modern Music*, to rebut the critics' narrowness. The literacy expatriates in Paris were in a similar position. Critics in traditional journals like the *Atlantic* and the *North American Review* were busy dismissing Hemingway, Sherwood Anderson, John dos Passos, et al. as mere misguided youth. The literati established their own little magazines, a service Minna Lederman performed for American musicians. Her journal gave experience to many young critics who would later gain wide acclaim, most notably Virgil Thomson. More importantly, she provided a forum where modern music and general issues in the arts were discussed objectively. Music criticism in *Modern Music*, like the literary discussions in *Broom*, the *Dial*, and *Seven Arts*, was not always sympathetic, but positive or negative, it did take a given work on its own terms.

There was some secessionism in all this activity, in contrast with Copland's and Nadia Boulanger's earlier views. But Copland found how rigidly the battle lines were drawn and had to adjust. He had tried to speak to a general audience with music that combined various elements of his experiences—the musical avant-garde, American popular music, his Jewish heritage, and his New York background. But to most listeners his music appeared too harsh or vulgar. He reacted, retreating to his own environment, and much of his music of the late twenties and early thirties reflects this withdrawal. He had tried to speak "with a largeness of utterance" which "would speak of universal things in a vernacular of American speech rhythms."²⁴ But by the late twenties, Copland discovered, "our search for musical ancestors had been abandoned or forgotten, partly, I suppose, because we became convinced that there were none."[25] Like the Great American Novel, Copland's "American music" now appeared elusive. With his quest behind him, he seemed adrift. One of his biographers characterized this time, which came with the decline in the nation's economy, as "bitter years."[26] Similarly, Wilfred Mellers described Copland as "expatriated and alienated."[27] Yet Copland reflected more optimistically:

> We were on our own, and something of the exhilaration that goes with being on one's own accompanied our very action. This self-reliant attitude was intensified by the open resistance to new music that was typical in the period after the First World War. . . . The fun of the fight against the musical philistines, the sorties and strategies, the converts won, and the hot arguments with dull-witted critics partly explain the particular excitement of that period. . . . It was an adventuresome time—a time when fresh resources had come to music and were being tested by a host of new composers with energy and ebullient spirits.[28]

The struggle with entrenched musical values was for Copland a challenge. As a composer "on his own" he turned inward to sources with which he felt comfortable. Symphonic jazz had little interest for him anymore.

A work of programmatic content of this period was *Vitebsk* (1929), a trio for piano, violin, and cello, subtitled "study on a Jewish theme." Several elements are at work in this beautiful piece. Clear is the Hebraic motif, with its distinction from traditional Western scales, which Copland highlighted with special markings, telling the violinist or cellist to play a quarter tone above ($\}$) or a quarter tone below ($\dot{c}$) the indicated note. Early in the piece Copland introduced the Hebraic theme in the violin and cello, with the piano banging a clangorous, bell-like accompaniment. With successions of major and minor chords and triads struck simultaneously, Copland enhanced the quarter-tone effect of his tuning indications. The microtonal and bell sounds effect a wailing-wall gathering. The piano part resembles the bell writing of Mussorgski in *Boris Godunov;* here Copland was perhaps symbolizing the Jewish-Russian conflict his ancestors had endured, for the piano part appears in conflict with the strings, a conflict resolved, reflecting Copland's biases, when the lyricism of the strings subdues the clangorous piano. Beyond the Russian-Jewish elements in *Vitebsk,* the rhythmic complexities reveal Stravinsky's continuing influence. The Parisian Neoclassicism may have reinforced Copland's affinity for Mussorgski and Russian music, materials he had encountered in Paris with Boulanger. Her conception of *grande ligne* had also abetted the free-flowing nature of the Hebraic theme he wished to develop. The French influence is most clear in the second section, where he presents a rapid lyrical theme, with a conjunct and chromatic melodic character that maintains the Hebraic mood, but with clarity and directness of harmony derived from the chamber music of Fauré. The piece then is Jewish in theme, French in manner.

Copland's reliance on French and Jewish materials reveals his own position as a composer in 1929. He was "on his own." His earlier enthusiasm for "American" music had subsided, and he was working in more isolation than in 1925. *Modern Music* was more important than the Boston or New York press; the Copland-Sessions concerts interested him more than the New York Philharmonic's. He was not bitter, but more distant. He had hoped he could awaken old music audiences at once to the value of American vernacular traditions and to the riches of modern compositional styles, and he never totally lost the hope. But meeting with little success, he had choices to make, and he believed first and foremost in the value of innovation. For, as Boulanger taught, to stand still is to decay. He was part of the modern world and could not leave it. Within that world he could write "American" music or any type of programmatic music. He could also write absolute music. The choice was his. "American" music seemed unattractive for the moment, like his "search for musical ancestors," a concept too amorphous to grasp. Turning inward, he felt at ease with Jewish themes, so he wrote *Vitebsk.* He also felt comfortable with most modern idioms, and for that reason, not from bitterness of alienation, he continued to write in acerbic, modern styles.

Ever since *The Cat and the Mouse* and the Passacaglia, Copland had shown interest in modern trends. His development in the twenties entailed an integration of modern styles with music of the various elements of his culture. By the time of *Vitebsk* he had achieved success. Further proof lies in the first movement, "Lento Molto," of Two Pieces for String Quartet. The second movement, "Rondino," was written in 1922, the first added in 1928. There is greater cohesiveness of materials in the "Lento Molto" than in the startling, often abrupt "Rondino" and a greater severity, created by textural leanness. This lean, acerbic style dominated Copland's music until 1934.

The major pieces of this acerbic period were Symphonic Ode (1928-1929), Variations for Piano (1930), Short Symphony (1932-1933), and Statements for Orchestra (1933-1934). The Symphonic Ode, like *Vitebsk*, is a transition piece, the last Copland would write on a grand scale until the late thirties. As with the Organ Symphony and Dance Symphony, there are sections thick in texture and virtuosic for the players, illustrating the continuing influence of Stravinsky, juxtaposed with jazz-like sections. The setting is similar to that of *Grogh*, but he had made great progress since then; the contrapuntal continuity is much stronger here than in similar juxtapositions in earlier work.

Copland's abandonment of grand-scale writing after the Symphonic Ode probably stemmed from his perception of success in fully coordinating the various elements permeating his music of the twenties into a large musical form. *Vitebsk* and "Lento Molto" illustrate a similar achievement in more intimate media. Meeting continued unfavorable criticism, Copland turned inward. *Vitebsk* illustrated one direction—toward his Hebraic roots. The Piano Variations, the Short Symphony, and the Orchestral Statements showed another—to the musical avant-garde. These three works are among his most technically complex. They reveal a matured composer, writing with complete mastery of the major styles of Western music, now not just French Neoclassicism but also, particularly in Piano Variations, the twelve-tone, serial methods of Arnold Schoenberg. Though outwardly aloof and acerbic, they still represent Copland's efforts to come to grips musically with his world. But in this case his scope was more limited, even more so than in *Vitebsk*. He had retreated from an American perspective, first to an Hebraic one and now to a personal one.

For such personal expression, serial techniques were logical. To various artists of the time, such as Schoenberg, James Joyce, and

Jean-Paul Sartre, seriality represented a system of expression to
order ideas in radically new fashions. In music, for example,
serial writing abandoned the parameters of traditional tonality.
It was not anarchy, though it might seem so to an uneducated ear.
It was a new form of order for a new time. Tonality could accommodate the pastoral yearnings of a Romantic symphonist but was
utterly incongruous for a twentieth-century urban composer. An
urbanite like Copland had to make personal sense of his environment. A pastoral setting results in artistic visions easily comprehensible to a popular audience. In a city, where the artist's vision
must be individual and abstract, the opposite is true. Surrounded by
so much that is synthetic, an artist need not, perhaps cannot,
literally reproduce his environment. A cubist painting is as synthetic
as a group of skyscrapers, and a twelve-tone musical piece as dissonant as the sound of the street. Wilfred Mellers wrote of Copland's
music at this time that it represented "the American Jew, expatriated
and alienated, [who] accepts the life of the big city and of machine-
made civilization."[29] Whether Copland felt expatriated and alienated
is debatable, since he generally was buoyantly optimistic. The
extent of his Jewish consciousness is also suspect, for there is little
evidence of it in his music after *Vitebsk*.

Mellers seems to see Copland's Jewish consciousness as bound to
alienation. But as the evidence for one breaks down, so does
the evidence for the other. Irving Howe's work demonstrates that
by the early thirties the American Jews of Copland's generation
had undergone a transformation in relations with the American
mainstream. To use but one example in politics: New York Jews,
according to Howe, were tied decreasingly to radicalism and
increasingly to liberalism, and thus readily joined the New York
Democratic party.[30] Howe's personal shift in this respect may
color his view of its applicability to his people. But to some degree
such a change did take place between 1920 and 1933, by which
time Jews were generally part of mainstream New York politics,
but not yet of American politics in general. That would come later.
In the same period, Copland passed through a similar state in his
artistic development. He had begun as a renegade with *The Cat
and the Mouse*. Then he learned the rigors of his craft, and they
led him, in the Passacaglia and the Organ Symphony, toward
absolute forms of composition. In the mid- and late twenties he
tried to unite the formal structures of his craft with elements of

American culture in *Music for the Theatre* and the Piano Concerto. Failure to achieve much public success led to a retreat back to absolute writing, seen by some critics as more anarchical, more radical, and to his Hebraic past, that is, to more limited cultural elements. Instead of in "America," Copland dwelt in the urban atmosphere which he knew. During this period, as did his fellow Jews in politics, he reconciled himself to New York. He had earlier attempted an accommodation of the more general aspects of American culture. He had failed. Now he would try again.

The political acculturation of the New York Jews, according to Howe, became complete during the time of Franklin Roosevelt and the New Deal, when traditional divisions between the New York Democratic party and much of the rest of the country weakened.[31] Copland shifted similarly in the mid- and late thirties. He sought to minimize the acerbic, aloof character of his music:

> During the mid-'30s I began to feel an increasing dissatisfaction with the relations of the music-loving public and the living composer. The old "special" public of the modern-music concerts had fallen away, and the conventional concert public continued apathetic or indifferent to anything but the established classics. It seemed to me that we composers were in danger of working in a vacuum. . . . I felt that it was worth the effort to see if I couldn't say what I had to say in the simplest possible terms.[32]

This self-conscious effort at simplicity was the genesis for such works as *Hear Ye! Hear Ye!* (1934), *El Salon Mexico* (1936), *Billy the Kid* (1938), *John Henry* (1940), *Lincoln Portrait* (1942), *Rodeo* (1942), *Fanfare for the Common Man* (1942), and *Appalachian Spring* (1944). Copland became a composer at last reconciled not just to New York, to Judaism, or to the avant-garde. He belonged to his country.

NOTES

1. See Hyman B. Grimstein, *The Rise of the Jewish Community in New York, 1654-1860* (Philadelphia: Jewish Publication Society of America, 1945), p. 223.

2. Hutchins Hapgood, *The Spirit of the Ghetto: Studies of the Jewish*

Quarter of New York (1902; reprint ed., New York: Funk and Wagnalls, 1965), pp. 246-47.

3. Ibid., pp. 254-55.

4. Ibid., p. 249.

5. Irving Howe, Selig Perlman Lecture, University of Wisconsin-Madison, May 5, 1977.

6. H. L. Mencken encapsuled the early twentieth-century views of America's intellectual ancestors when he wrote: "A Puritan is someone deathly afraid that somewhere someone is happy." Many noted scholars shared his perception, including James Truslow Adams, *The Founding of New England* (Boston: Atlantic Monthly Press, 1921), and Vernon L. Parrington, *Main Currents in American Thought*, vol. 1, *The Colonial Mind, 1620-1800* (New York: Harcourt, Brace and Co., 1930). In the twenties and thirties began the more thorough, matured views—Carl Becker, *Beginnings of the American People* (New York: Houghton Mifflin Co., 1915) and *The United States: An Experiment in Democracy* (New York: Harper and Brothers, 1920), Kenneth B. Murdock, *Increase Mather: The Foremost American Puritan* (Cambridge: Harvard University Press, 1925); Charles Beard, *History of the United States* (New York: Macmillan, 1931) and *The American Spirit* (New York: Macmillan, 1942), Samuel Eliot Morison, *Builders of the Bay Colony* (Boston: Houghton Mifflin, The Riverside Press, 1930) and Perry Miller, *Orthodoxy in Massachusetts* (Cambridge: Harvard University Press, 1933) and *The New England Mind: The Seventeenth Century* (Cambridge: Harvard University Press, 1954).

7. Irene Heskes, ed., *Studies in Jewish Music: Collected Writings of A. W. Binder* (New York: Bloch Publishing Co., 1971), pp. 210-12.

8. Copland, *The New Music, 1900-1960*, p. 151.

9. Ibid., p. 152.

10. Irving Howe, *World of Our Fathers* (New York: Simon and Schuster, 1976), pp. 357-59.

11. Copland, *The New Music*, p. 153.

12. Ibid., p. 154.

13. Ibid.

14. Ibid., p. 155.

15. Aaron Copland, "Gabriel Fauré: A Neglected Master," *Musical Quarterly*, October 1924, pp. 573-86.

16. Copland, *Copland on Music*, pp. 88-89.

17. Howe, *World of Our Fathers*, pp. 492-93.

18. Rosenfeld, *An Hour with American Music*, p. 133.

19. Philip Hale, *Boston Herald*, January 29, 1927, p. 31.

20. Henry T. Parker, *Boston Evening Transcript*, February 4, 1927, p. 13.

21. Aaron Copland letter to Nicolas Slonimsky, February 10, 1927, in Nicolas Slonimsky, ed., *Music Since 1900* (New York: Charles Scribner's Sons, 1971), p. 445.

22. Copland, *Copland on Music*, p. 98.

23. Copland, *The New Music*, p. 157.

24. Copland, *Music and Imagination*, p. 111.

25. Ibid., p. 113.

26. Arnold Dobrin, *Aaron Copland, His Life and Times* (New York: Thomas Y. Crowell Co., 1927), pp. 108-19.

27. Mellers, *Music in a New Found Land*, p. 84.

28. Copland, *Music and Imagination*, p. 113.

29. Mellers, *Music in a New Found Land*, p. 84.

30. Howe, *World of Our Fathers*, pp. 386-87.

31. Ibid. pp. 392-93.

32. Copland, *The New Music*, p. 160.

CODA

In 1900, amidst the ferment of the United States's "coming of age," Macmillan and Company Publishers wanted to present volume-length histories of the various arts in America. When musicians and critics were approached for the volume on music, many tossed off the idea as impractical, since there was "not enough" American music to warrant full monographic treatment. This perception of America's musical poverty by many of the nation's major music figures arose from cultural dislocations which were to take many years to resolve. Many Americans simply were blind to their vernacular traditions, and indeed much of this vernacular music had not been, and still is not, notated or recorded. Nevertheless, some of the blindness stemmed from elitism. It was unthinkable for many to consider the songs of Southern blacks or urban ethnic groups—"the sweepings of our streets"[1]—as on equal footing with a Brahms symphony. The "street" metaphor was significant. If filth could not be swept away, city officials in early twentieth-century America tried to cordon it off into specific areas. In such cities as New Orleans and Kansas City these areas became infested with crime, disease, drugs, prostitution—and jazz.

The composer Béla Bartók was one of the major twentieth-century figures to advocate linking various folk and art traditions. While some musicians wanted to keep the musical streets "well swept," Bartók saw life, musical and otherwise, more organically. He once thus described a manure pile:

> There is life in this dried-up mound of dung. . . . You
> see . . . how the worms and bugs are working busily
> helping themselves to whatever they need, making
> little tunnels and passages, and then soil enters, bringing
> with it stray seeds. Soon pale shoots of grass will appear,
> and life will complete its cycle.[2]

Bartók understood the poverty in an art that disdainfully isolated itself from its cultural components, but many Americans in the
late nineteenth and early twentieth centuries did not share his
wisdom.

From colonial times distinctions of genre had existed in American
music, distinctions that corresponded to more general social
and economic divisions. Yet in the musical activity before the
American Civil War, ideas and methods were shared between
various genres, if only because the size of the musical world was
small in the colonial and early national years. By 1865, however,
the American music world had grown. Then two things simultaneously occurred: composers in significant numbers began going to
study in Europe, and the lines between the elite and nonelite in
America hardened. The art music world no longer engaged in
"vertical" interaction with American vernacular culture but greatly
intensified its "horizontal" communication with the art music of
Germany and later of France, countries where Americans studied.

But the separation of art and vernacular music could not be
maintained. Many German and French musicians with whom
Americans worked mined their own vernacular resources. With
such new inventions as the nickelodeon, the player piano, and the
phonograph, American vernacular materials became increasingly
available by 1900 and fewer art musicians could plead ignorance of
them. Finally, foreign musicians, particularly the French, began
using American materials in their compositions. The contradiction
of an American culture, disdainful of its vernacular heritage,
seeking to be as polished as Europe while some Europeans enjoyed
and respected jazz grew more and more apparent. Art and vernacular strands began to join.

After long neglect, vernacularists like Roy Harris reacted to
the new state of things with a kind of anti-elite elitism, perhaps a

musical populism. As the fad for the primitive in part swelled the popularity of the vernacular traditions in postwar Europe, composers like George Antheil catapulted themselves to fame, and even Virgil Thomson could occasionally be seduced by the fad. For Aaron Copland, whose personal vernacular, a complicated combination of Jewish, New York, and, later, American motifs, lay a bit outside the national mainstream, the confluence of vernacular and art music traditions showed him a way to go. Other Americans moved in diverse directions: Romanticism, Impressionism, Neoclassicism, polytonality, atonalism, expressionism, nationalism, and often some combination of these.

The removal of barriers between genres engendered great diversity that demanded and received control and direction from Vincent d'Indy and Nadia Boulanger. Their efforts saved most Americans from fads and eclecticism.

With this diversity, the question of American identity remained, indeed still remains, vexing. "The way to write American music is simple," said Virgil Thomson in his typical cavalier fashion. "All you have to do is be an American and then write any kind of music you wish. There is precedent and model here for all the kinds. And any Americanism worth bothering about is everybody's property anyway. Leave it to the unconscious; let nature speak."[3] Letting "nature speak" was not so easy for many twentieth-century composers, however. With the rise of totalitarianism in various European nations, all the arts fell increasingly under imposed official control. Composers in the Soviet Union and Nazi Germany had to follow imposed aesthetic percepts or be unable to follow their profession, or worse. Amidst the polarization of politics, social mores, and aesthetics in Europe, the United States became the major music center of the West, where Europeans flocked and free expression continued. As a result, by 1945 the United States was the main battleground for the music world's sorties. Replacing Europe, the United States needed an established tradition of excellence with composers who would maintain their indentities. It needed to avoid being engulfed by the European traditions which came over with Schoenberg, Krenek, Stravinsky, Bartók, Hindemith, Weill, and Milhaud. The presence of these men was not overwhelming, for American musical culture had become secure. It had grown to maturity out of its pre-Civil War infancy, through its occasionally precocious childhood under German authority, from which it had rebelled, and then its college and graduate school years in France.

The musically ebullient decade of the thirties brought American music to a new level of maturity. Jazz grew more and more popular and less ghettoized by the musical establishment. The decade saw great expansion in the radio and recording industries and an unprecedented proliferation of orchestras. All this, plus the performances and scholarship of the New Deal's Works Progress Administration Music Project, brought new quantities of music to an expanding audience. As music became more pervasive and legitimate, self-consciousness at being a musician, which had greatly affected such different artists as Harris, Ives, and Parker, began to disappear. American musicians easily adapted to new genres and developed interesting innovations in such old ones as opera, ballet, and symphony. Thomson's *Four Saints in Three Acts*, Copland's *Rodeo*, and Harris's Symphony no. 3 are examples. Taking jazz and blues out of the ghetto and introducing modern innovations in both old and new genres led to a further mixing of styles. Artists like Duke Ellington, who had never cared for the label jazz, employed some of the harmonies of the impressionists. Copland and Thomson borrowed freely from a variety of American vernacular idioms. This merging of heretofore separate genres was pronounced in new musical fields like film, where nineteenth-century cultural traditions and self-consciousness of expression and form did not easily take hold. Earlier, piano accompanists for silent films had also moved freely between the traditionally separate art and vernacular genres. This is not to say that American music could only come from a merger of art and vernacular musics. But earlier American music had difficulty establishing identity with all the barriers between genres. When the barriers crumbled, single genres came forth without a sense of (self-) imposed isolation, and various combinations occurred. It was often the combination of vernacular idioms with art music forms that placed American materials in an internationally recognizable language.

In the thirties it was hoped that economic hardship might bring about revolutionary changes. This did not happen. Critics from the left, and others, have since examined the time and the years preceding to find out why not. These examinations touched on music. American composers' continued use of such European forms as ballet, opera, and symphony smacked of elitism, and critics blamed the music world of Paris where Americans studied. For example, Sidney Finkelstein, a prolific writer on the arts and society, wrote of

> the school of thought [in Paris] which lumped together the classic heritage of Beethoven and the latest romanticism of Wagner as one great body of "outmoded" music, and hailed the "return" to the eighteenth century and the return to the artisan spirit of feudalism as "progress." The result is a narrowness of experience and range of feeling in . . . music, a tendency to let the instrumental sound dominate and thus constrict the entire musical conception, all in the name of "clarity" and "form." There seems to be a constant fear that to break out into a genuinely dramatic experience, to represent the real conflicts of life, to search for singing, lyrical qualities, would be thought "old-fashioned" and even vulgar. . . . [The] entire [Paris] generation of American composers . . . suffered from this fundamental error of regarding formalistic systems or a borrowing from feudalism as a "liberation" of American music.[4]

Finkelstein saw a dichotomy between adherence to clarity and form on the one hand and genuinely dramatic expression on the other, and he asserted that composers clung to Classical forms out of a "fear" of experiencing their feelings. But the writing of a symphony is not a mere intellectual exercise, and instrumental music has no less inherent feeling than vocal. Finkelstein based his critique on a popular conception of pre-Romantic, Classical music as lacking in emotional intensity. He asserted that in the twenties French and American musicians had turned away from most German music, from Beethoven to Wagner, and resurrected earlier composers, thus equating Romanticism with nationalism and feeling and Classicism with artistic stoicism. He correctly pointed out that nineteenth-century composers, particularly the more nationalistic Germans, ranked low in postwar Paris. But here politics were as responsible as any musical consideration, since Russian, Polish, Italian, English, and French composers of Romantic styles, including French Wagnerians, remained popular. Nevertheless, pre-Romantic traits such as thinner textures, shorter works, and aprogrammatic forms did become dominant. Historically these traits imply no more emotional content but no less. They generally have less programmatic content, which renders their emotionalism less overt, less accessible. But this does not mean that the composers feared to show their feelings. Indeed, one reason for the anti-Romantic turn in the twenties was a perception that the emotional content of late nineteenth-century music was so grandiose as to be puerile. As a matter of fact, the style of Wagner can be mimed as easily as can Haydn's; Finkelstein, however, succumbed to the popular fallacy that Haydn's music lacks feeling. Romantic composers had asserted that eighteenth-century music became too rational. This happens, of course, with virtually any artistic style which stays too long in vogue and becomes institutionalized. It happened to the symphonic style of the Romantic era.

Perhaps Finkelstein saw Romantic music more favorably because it spoke to a wider and less elitist audience than did the music of the Classical era. The social makeup of audiences that heard Mozart's symphonies, however, was of no concern to Parisian Neoclassicists. It was the musical qualities which attracted them. Finkelstein blurred the lines between audience and composer and overstated the degree to which the form of a piece may dictate its content; this happens only with a composer of mediocre talent and training. Nadia Boulanger herself feared students might be taken in by the trendiness of an avant-garde technique or form. Such mimicry seemed as sterile to her as to Finkelstein.

Turning specifically to Nadia Boulanger, the music critic and historian Andre Hodeir wrote with disapproval of the aesthetic conservatism inherent in the formalism of her pedagogy and in the more general Neoclassical aesthetic.[5] Her association with Stravinsky, in view of the latter's cool relationship with the Soviet Union and willingness to give concerts in Germany and Italy as late as 1938, supported Hodeir's evaluation of the Parisian American, of Nadia Boulanger, and of Neoclassicism. A more fundamentally radical approach to music, Hodeir felt, was that of atonalists like Schoenberg and Krenek. Atonalists in music, like the left in politics, seemed to claim that a principal mainspring of expression dominant since the Renaissance, tonality in music and capitalism in political economy, had become impoverished and should be replaced, not with anarchy but with a new structure suited to the times. In contrast with revolutionary atonality, Parisian Neoclassicism was a dead end. These traditions seemed, further, too close to the old elite traditions of Europe, devotion to which had delayed American composers' development of a national consciousness.

Such criticism is tenuous. First, Schoenberg, according to himself, was not a revolutionary. Nor did he view his system as revolutionary, though leftist aestheticians chose to. Second, tinges of formalism in Neoclassicism imply no disdain for emotion in music. Stravinsky, Tchaikovsky, and Glinka, as well as Schumann and Brahms, believed in its value. Indeed, they felt that formal structures were needed so emotions could speak in perpetuity, not merely for the moment to a circle of friends. Furthermore, Nadia Boulanger's dislike of the serialism Hodeir preferred stemmed from her belief that a young composer could write in that style in a coldly cerebral fashion, ignoring feelings, which provided the only genuine source of musical expression. The heart, she felt, was the source of creation, and if a person like George Gershwin could create by following his feelings without having any great knowledge of the formal procedures of composition, she could view it as a miracle and accept it. The unmiraculous majority, however, needed rigorous training to give comprehensible form to their feelings. Thus Boulanger did not separate intuition and formal training; for all but a select few the two were inextricably intertwined.

To Hodeir and Finkelstein, the increasing torpor of the main musical styles of the eighteenth and nineteenth century revealed the impoverishment of the aesthetics of the age. Hodeir wanted composers to pursue atonalism. Finkelstein preferred emphasis on lyrical, singing music. The freshness of some of the music of the Parisian Neoclassicists, however, shows that the judgment of Neoclassicism as a dead end was an exaggeration. Though the leftists' link between musical and political judgments may have some merit, their inaccuracy in overstating the impoverishment of Neoclassicism and the Paris school are akin to their previous failure to see how far the capitalist world (Germany in the 1880s and England and the United States in the early twentieth century) would yield to social protest and meet, or give the impression of meeting, some of the demands for social reform. The "forces of oppression" were more flexible and hence their staying power was greater and more dangerous than many leftists had reckoned. Even in the thirties capitalist power had more life than the leftists thought. What they thought of as its musical appendage did, too. Finkelstein and Hodeir criticized the formalism of the Paris-schooled Americans as perpetuating the rigid structure which oppressed vernacular genres. The interaction in the thirties between the art music world and the vernacular belied this view, as did corporate America's acceptance of some social welfare programs. Like their brethren in social and political criticism, Hodeir and Finkelstein thus found that the events of the thirties undercut some of their criticism. They felt betrayed. Like the political revolution to which, in their minds, it was tied, their aesthetic revolution never came, in part because some of their criticisms were met. Jazz and popular song gained musicological respectability, and the art music world relented from its stiff formalism far more than its critics had thought possible.

The Paris generation was attacked by the left for not confronting "the real conflicts of life." It did so, but not as the left wanted. Leftists would have preferred that composers toss the vestiges of art music into the trash and embrace modern, serial modes of expression. A few Americans—Marc Blitzstein, Lou Harrison, and Merton Brown—did this, as did many European émigrés, but most did not. In the thirties most American composers transcended formalism and art for art's sake and confronted "the real conflicts of life" by seeking to integrate elements in formerly separate worlds. From a leftist perspective, they showed themselves liberals, not leftists.

Of the New Deal, a historian wrote that for any who hoped for a fundamental restructuring of the nation's economic and political institutions "the New Deal was not a promise betrayed, it was essentially misdirected from the beginning."[6] Similarly, American musicians as they emerged in the thirties did not betray the left. With few exceptions they had never intended to follow in the directions it prescribed. In that sense an American musical identity did emerge in the thirties. It was an identity of collective enterprise that in curious and often subtle ways extended out of models in Europe but ultimately failed to parallel the lines of activity there. Out of European events social critics developed modes of aesthetic analysis. These modes, lacking proper adaptors, short-circuited when plugged into the American scene. The elusive adaptor is the key to American music's uniqueness.

The emergence of a unique and mature American musical character in the thirties ended the identity crisis of American musicians. Composers and critics no longer needed to bemoan diversity, for America was diverse. They accepted the fact and accordingly composers could borrow freely from their past, or from anywhere else, with little fear of derision. They need only to be sincere and technically competent. Their predecessors in nineteenth-century Germany had been both, but also self-consciously anationalistic, so much so that their posture had been, in Copland's words, "overgentlemanly" in demeanor. Many successful Americans opposed the Germanics' disdain for anything that smacked of vernacularism, but did so with equal posturing. Where the Germanics were elitists, their successors were equally elitist as populists.

It was the generation of Copland and Thomson, following the early twentieth-century Americanists, which provided an answer. They developed technical acumen, as had the Germanics, and a consciousness of themselves as Americans. The Germanics had showed the necessity of technical training. Some early twentieth-century Americanists, in their inadequacies, revealed it counterfactually. In the twenties Americans went to Paris, learned their trade, and learned it well. Paris also provided them a work environment free of old sectional/cosmopolitan tensions. There Americans could sort themselves out within an environment familiar, since it was Western, yet not too familiar, since France was the one European country from which stemmed few American lineages. There young American musicians, like their counterparts in other arts, could focus on art for art's sake within the sweep of Western culture, free from old debates and parochialism. Thus as they matured, a collective identity emerged among Americans released from past posturings either for or against Americanism. Composers could be as nationalistic as Roy Harris or as absolute as Walter

Piston. Roots existed in American music for virtually any type of expression, and the competing vestiges of the musical past now added up to something. American music had historical definition. As a result the music that developed in the thirties and early forties—Thomson's music from *The River* and *The Plow That Broke the Plains* and Copland's *Rodeo* and *Appalachian Spring*— emerged, and remains, as music for a wide cross-section of Americans.

After 1945 the forces of pluralism and commercialism stole most social basis from artistic culture, making any further forging of a national music virtually impossible. We had it, briefly. Perhaps another Nadia Boulanger will appear who can help us find it again.

NOTES

1. Daniel Gregory Mason, *The Dilemma of American Music*, p. 140.

2. Agatha Fassett, *Béla Bartók's American Years: The Naked Face of Genius* (Boston: Houghton Mifflin, 1958), p. 3.

3. *New York Herald Tribune*, January 25, 1948, section 5, p. 8.

4. Sidney Finkelstein, *How Music Expresses Ideas* (New York: International Publishers, 1952), pp. 115-16.

5. Andre Hodeir, *Since Debussy: A View of Contemporary Music*, translated by Noel Burch (New York: Grove Press, 1961), p. 222.

6. Paul Conkin, *The New Deal*, rev. ed. (Arlington Heights, Ill.: AHM Publishing Corporation, 1975), p. 101.

ESSAY
ON SOURCES

Studies in the history of music tend to fall into two major categories. The first is basically ahistorical—focusing on the notes and the artists' expression of ideas, disregarding the period when the music was written aside from merely pointing out the dates of composition. The second—a narration of the historical circumstances of musical phenomenon—comprises what I call the "what Beethoven ate for breakfast" approach. Works of this latter sort, by themselves, tell one little about music, only about the extramusical events in the lives of musicians. The first category is blind; the second is deaf. There are many great blind musicians; no deaf ones, Ezra Pound notwithstanding. The deaf approach, like any narrative, tends to be simple. Sensitivity to the musical irrelevance of such "history" has led some musicians to champion the first approach. The best book, for example, on the music of the late eighteenth and early nineteenth century, Charles Rosen's *The Classical Style* (New York: Viking Press, 1971), begins by denying most historical analysis. The key features of the music of the time, to Rosen, are three great figures—Haydn, Mozart, and Beethoven—whose music he then analyzes. This discussion is not meant to belittle Rosen. Indeed, I choose him to illustrate the profound levels an essentially ahistorical approach to music can attain. And Rosen himself is not exclusively a musician. He has written on such diverse subjects as Beaudelaire and basketball. Historical analysis has seemed impoverished. But some bad history does not mean that historical analysis has no value to a musician. The fact that music exists as sound produced over time makes it part of history. As such it can be analyzed historically as well as musically, and in both cases poorly or well.

Rosen's rejection of history probably stemmed from his encounter with the frustrations that many have felt in trying to come to grips with the eighteenth century and the Enlightenment. If there were philosophical elements, beyond the most nebulous, which bound that era together, no one has yet been able to articulate them. Interesting along these lines is that in its excellent series of volumes on music history, W. W. Norton has yet to present a volume on the Classical era. Gustave Reese's volumes—*Music in the Middle Ages* (New York: W. W. Norton, 1940) and *Music in the Renaissance* (New York: W. W. Norton, 1959)—and Manfred Bukofzer's *Music of the Baroque Era* (New York: W. W. Norton, 1947) are excellent studies of the music and generally acceptable summations of the aesthetic precepts that underlay the music of those times. Alfred Einstein's *Music in the Romantic Era* (New York: W. W. Norton, 1947) and William Austin's *Music in the Twentieth Century* (New York: W. W. Norton, 1966), though superb on the music, are less convincing as total statements of the aesthetics of their respective times. But no one really expects any such historical synthesis of music, or of any other art, after 1800. On the other hand, we still seem to think the eighteenth century has relatively monolithic meaning. The reluctance among the scholars of the eighteenth century that Norton approached indicates that our conception of when pluralism seems to have taken hold in Western society needs to be pushed back in time.

Aside from Rosen, the general rejection of history applied to music more simply extends from the nonartistic quality of some widely read histories of music. Few care what Beethoven ate. If his food had anything to do with his music, no one has yet demonstrated it. But Beethoven's relationship to Kant, Goethe, Schiller, and Fichte is important for a full understanding of him as an artist. Thus the question is not whether to analyze music historically but how it is done. The study of the music of the past as an extension of the history of ideas is the third category of music history, one that is woefully incomplete. Intellectual historians who expertly comment on various arts from philosophy to painting to poetry often balk at integrating music into their work. There are two principal reasons for this. One needs to possess some knowledge of the language of musical notation, and music itself tends more toward absolute expression than do other arts.

Despite the heritage of opposition between music and history, some writers have tried to study music as an extension of the history of ideas. A historian who, despite some rather arcane sensibilities, has been rather successful at it for many years is Jacques Barzun, particularly in *Berlioz and the Romantic Century*, third edition (New York: Columbia University Press, 1969), and in *Romanticism and the Modern Ego* (Boston: Little, Brown, 1943). Three musicologists—Ernst Newman, Romain Rolland, and Paul Henry Lang—transcended the normal bounds of their field and revealed in virtually all their writings a keen sensitivity to related contemporaneous events. Some of the best examples were Lang's *Music in Western Civilization* (New York: W. W. Norton, 1941) and *Problems of Modern Music*, which he edited (New York: W. W. Norton, 1960); Rolland's *Musicians of Today*, translated by Mary Blaiklock (New York: Henry Holt, 1928); Newman's *The Life of Richard Wagner* (New York: Alfred A. Knopf, 1933), *From the World of Music: Essays from the London Sunday Times* (New York: Coward-McCann, 1957), *More Essays from the London Sunday Times* (New York: Coward-McCann, 1958); and Herbert van Thal, ed., *Testament of Music: Essays and Papers by Ernst Newman* (London: Putnam, 1962).

In the related field of aesthetics, some of the more stimulating discussions can be found in the following: Gilbert Chase, *Two Lectures in the Form of a Pair:* "Music, Culture, and History" and "Structuralism and Music" (New York: Institute for Studies in American Music, Brooklyn College, 1973); Carlos Chavez, *Musical Thought* (Cambridge: Harvard University Press, 1961); Igor Stravinsky, *Poetics of Music* (Cambridge: Harvard University Press, 1970); and Leonard Bernstein, *The Unanswered Question* (Cambridge: Harvard University Press, 1976).

General cultural studies of nineteenth- and twentieth-century Europe often contain analytical models which, though the writer may not know it, apply directly to contemporaneous events in music. Thus many such works have proven useful: George Mosse, *The Culture of Western Europe* (New York: Rand McNally and Co., 1965); Gerhard Masur, *Prophets of Yesterday: Studies in European*

Culture, 1890-1914 (New York: Macmillan Co., 1961); Karl Mannheim, *Man and Society in the Age of Reason* (London: Kegan Paul, Trench, Trubner and Co., 1935); Arthur O. Lovejoy, *Essays in the History of Ideas* (Baltimore: Johns Hopkins University Press, 1948), and *The Great Chain of Being* (Cambridge: Harvard Univeristy Press, 1933); and H. Stuart Hughes, *Consciousness and Society, The Reorientation of European Social Thought, 1890-1930* (New York: Alfred A. Knopf, 1958).

On the American scene several works can be similarly employed: Henry F. May, *The End of American Innocence: A Study of the First Years of Our Time* (Chicago: Quadrangle Books, 1964); Henry Steele Commager, *The American Mind: An Interpretation of American Thought and Character Since the 1880's* (New Haven: Yale University Press, 1950); Merle Curti, *The Growth of American Thought*, third edition (New York: Harper and Row Publishers, 1964); Leslie Fiedler, *The End to Innocence: Essays on Culture and Politics* (Boston: Beacon Press, 1955); and Richard Hofstadter, *Anti-Intellectualism in American Life* (New York: Alfred A. Knopf, 1963). Three older works of this sort were also useful in their illuminating conceptions of the "American character" in the minds of people who were contemporaries of the musicians studied in these essays: Clayton Sedgwick Cooper, *American Ideals* (Garden City, N.Y.: Doubleday, Page and Co., 1916); Bernard Faÿ, *The American Experiment* (New York: Harcourt, Brace and Co., 1929); and Edwin Mims, *Adventurous America, A Study of Contemporary Life and Thought* (New York: Charles Scribner's Sons, 1929).

Reversing the flow from history to music, there are many great works on various segments of the history of Western music to which historians can apply their analyses. William Austin's *Music in the Twentieth Century* (New York: W. W. Norton and Co., 1966) is the best general account of contemporary music. It is remarkably comprehensive, though Austin is much stronger on pre-1945 developments than on those following the Second World War; he sometimes tries to bring more order to the chaotic stylistic relationships between various movements than actually existed. Marion Bauer's *Twentieth-Century Music, How It Developed, How to Listen to It* (New York: G. P. Putnam's Sons, 1933) is a historically oriented interpretation of the music of the first three decades of the twentieth century. Bauer herself is a composer of less innovative bent than such individuals as Stravinsky, Schoenberg, and Bartók. Feeling herself "in the middle" esthetically between the avant-garde and most listeners, she tries to explain the moderns by tracing roots back to the more readily comprehensible composers of the nineteenth century. The book is indeed helpful to many listeners of modern music. But, because much twentieth-century music stems from sources outside the realm of nineteenth-century art music, some of her analyses are a bit distorted. In *Paths to Modern Music* (New York: Scribner's, 1971), Lawrence Davies tries much the same thing, emphasizing the continuing influence of Romantic traditions in this century, much as Arthur O. Lovejoy did in the more general realm of cultural history. Davies places great emphasis on the importance of Wagner, perhaps too great an emphasis.

Wilfred Mellers, in *Man and His Music: Romanticism in the Twentieth Century* (New York: Schocken Books, 1962), traces the continuing threads of Romanticism (which he unfortunately virtually equates with nationalism) as sensitively as Davies but spends as much time on the negation of the Romantic impulse in twentieth-century music. Davies sees Wagner's influence as pivotal in the rise of English music in the twentieth century, through Vaughan Williams, Elgar, and Britten. Yet the music of these composers extended as much from the "rediscovery" of fifteenth- and sixteenth-century English masters as from Wagner. This unearthing of neglected music was very important in the rise of many national musics in this century, as revealed in the pedagogical activity of Nadia Boulanger and Vincent d'Indy. A very good series of essays that explores the impact, both positive and negative, of such rediscovery is William Hays, ed., *Twentieth-Century Views of Music History* (New York: Scribner's, 1972). Other interesting interpretive schemes are H. H. Stuckenschmidt, *Twentieth-Century Music* (New York: McGraw Hill, 1967), and Jim Samson, *Music in Transition: A Study in Tonal Expansion and Atonality* (New York: W. W. Norton, 1977), which trace developments through some basic elements of music—rhythm, pitch, timbre, harmony, form— and what composers have done with them, and Donald Mitchell, *The Language of Modern Music* (New York: St. Martin's Press,

1970), in which the author traces musical developments in relationship with the other arts, particularly painting. The latter contains some of the best material on post-1945 events.

Many works exist that fit into the ahistorical category. Unencumbered by any interpretive scheme, they examine the notes on the page, composer by composer, and provide useful data for the historian: Paul Collaer, *A History of Modern Music*, translated from the French by Sally Abeles (New York: World Publishing Co., 1961); Otto Deri, *Exploring Twentieth-Century Music* (New York: Holt, Rinehart, and Winston, 1968); Peter Hanson, *An Introduction to Twentieth-Century Music*, third edition (Boston: Allyn and Bacon, 1971); Joseph Machlis, *Introduction to Contemporary Music* (New York: W. W. Norton, 1961); F. W. Sternfeld, ed., *Music in the Modern Age* (London: Weidenfeld and Nicolson, 1973); and Peter Yates, *Twentieth-Century Music* (New York: Minerva Press, 1967).

Several works that focused on the French scene proved most useful. One of the finest and most enjoyable books on Paris is Roger Shattuck's *The Banquet Years: The Origins of the Avant Garde in France, 1885 to World War I*, revised edition (New York: Vintage Books, 1968). Shattuck deals capably with music as well as with other arts here, so his book does not give one the feeling of visiting a string of artistic ghettos. Further, he writes of the late nineteenth and early twentieth century as a continuum, in contrast with so many historians and musicians who seem tyrannized by the chronological switch from nineteenth to twentieth century. On French music specifically, the works of Martin Cooper: *French Music From the Death of Berlioz to the Death of Fauré* (London: Oxford University Press, 1951) and *Georges Bizet* (Westport, Conn.: Greenwood Press, 1971); those of James Harding: *Erik Satie* (New York: Praeger Publishers, 1975), *Gounod* (London: George Allen and Unwin, 1973), *Massenet* (London: J. M. Dent, 1970), *Saint-Saëns and His Circle* (London: Chapman Hall, 1965), and *The Ox on the Roof: Scenes from the Musical Life in Paris in the Twenties* (London: McDonald and Co., 1972); and Edwin Evans's translation of G. Jean-Aubry's *French Music Today* (London: Kegan Paul, Trench, Trubner, and Co., 1929) are the best in the English language. All are musicologically sound and reveal great sensitivity to the interpersonal relations and rivalries that were very much a part of the French music scene in these years. Camille Saint-Saëns himself wrote about music life with the same lucidity apparent in his music: *Outspoken Essays on Music* (London: Kegan, Paul, Trench, Trubner and Co., Ltd., 1922) and *Musical Memories*, translated by Gile Rich (London: John Murray and Co., 1921). The sources in the French language are strictly musical, tracing music composer by composer: René Dumesnil, *La Musique Contemporaine en France* (Paris: Librairie Armand Colin, 1930) and *La musique en France entre les deux guerres, 1919-1939* (Geneva: Editions du Milieu du Monde, 1940); R. Bernard, *Les Tendances de la Musique Française Moderne* (Paris: Editions Durand et Fils, 1930); and Julien Tiersot, *Un Demi-Siecle de Musique Française, 1870-1919* (Paris: Librairie Felix Alcan, 1925). Several biographies of the two major figures in French music in these years—Claude Debussy and Maurice Ravel—provide much information beyond the narrative of each's life and music: Maurice Dumesnil, *Claude Debussy: Master of Dreams* (New York: Ives Washburn, 1940); Stefan Jarocinski, *Debussy, Impressionism and Symbolism*, translated by Rollo Myers (London: Ernst Eulenberg, 1976); Edward Lockspeiser, *Debussy, His Life and Mind*, two volumes (London: Cassell and Co., Ltd., 1962); Oscar Thompson, *Debussy, Man and Artist* (New York: Tudor Publishing Co., 1940); Léon Vallas, *Claude Debussy: His Life and Works*, translated by Marie O'Brien and Grace O'Brien (London: Oxford University Press, 1933); Norman Demuth, *Ravel* (London: J. M. Dent, 1947); Rollo Myers, *Ravel: His Life and Works* (New York: Thomas Yoseloff, 1960); Roger Nichols, *Ravel* (London: J. M. Dent, 1977); Arbie Orenstein, *Ravel, Man and Musician* (New York: Columbia University Press, 1975); Victor Seroff, *Maurice Ravel* (New York: Henry Holt and Company, 1953); and H. H. Stuckenschmidt, *Maurice Ravel: Variations on His Life and Work*, translated by Samuel Rosenbaum (London: Calder and Boyars, 1969).

A problem with so many of these sources, except Shattuck, is that the place of music in the intellectual milieu of Paris is never made clear. The tendency to ghettoize or ignore music crops up in many of the works on the general intellectual life of Paris, in the twenties and in other times. While secondary sources on intellectual or cultural history can be "plugged in" to the musical scene, many of the works on the twenties by people who were there have to be taken on their own terms. The following, among others, certainly create a lively vision for the reader of that era: Daniel Aaron, *Writers on the Left* (New York: Harcourt, Brace and World, 1961); Frederick J. Hoffman, *The Twenties: American Writing in the Post-War Decade* (New York: Viking Press, 1955); Malcolm Cowley, *Exiles Return* (New York: Viking Press, 1951); Bernard DeVoto, *The Literary Fallacy* (Boston: Little, Brown and Co., 1944); Ernest Earnest, *The Single Vision: The Alienation of American Intellectuals* (New York: New York University Press, 1970); Anthony C. Hilfer, *The Revolt from the Village, 1915-1930* (Chapel Hill: University of North Carolina Press, 1969); and Warren Fansch, ed., *The Twenties, Fiction, Poetry, Drama* (Deland, Fla.: Everett Edwards, 1975). From them, however, music seems, in comparison with most other arts, off on its own. A few contemporaneous accounts deal with music: Janet Flanner, *An American in Paris* (New York: Simon and Schuster, 1940), and George Wickes, *Americans in Paris* (1939; reprint ed., Garden City, N. Y.: Doubleday and Co., 1969). Ezra Pound's and Gertrude Stein's writings certainly reveal music to have been central to their artistic lives. Ezra Pound's writings on music have been completely collected in R. Murray Schafer, ed., *Ezra Pound on Music* (New York: New Directions Publishing Corporation, 1977). The best account of Gertrude Stein's activity, besides that revealed in her own writings, is in James R. Mellow, *Charmed Circle: Gertrude Stein and Company* (New York: Praeger Publishers, 1974). The question, Was music peripheral compared to the other arts of the Left Bank? still remains open. Perhaps music's absence from many of the reminiscences of the literati merely indicates certain technical inadequacies in their schooling that kept them from dealing with music in the same depth to which they could go when discussing other arts. Those who had greater knowledge of or enthusiasm for music, like Stein and Pound, show that the hotly fought aesthetic issues of the day had many manifestations in music. The writings of the musicians themselves show music deeply embedded in the activities of the Left Bank: Vernon Duke, *Passport to Paris* (Boston: Little, Brown, 1955); Virgil Thomson, *Virgil Thomson* (New York: Alfred A. Knopf, 1966); George Antheil, *Bad Boy of Music* (Garden City, N. Y.: Doubleday, Doran and Co., 1945); Igor Stravinsky, *Autobiography* (New York: Simon and Schuster, 1936); and

Aaron Copland, *The New Music*, rev. ed. (New York: W.W. Norton, 1968). The magazines of Paris, *Broom* and *Transatlantic Review*, do not resolve this ambivalence either. Music was present, in the magazines and in Paris, but it remains unclear whether or not music was an equal combatant in the artistic sorties of Paris or, like Nadia Boulanger's studio and the American Conservatory at Fontainebleau, slightly away from the center of things.

The technical aspects of music, which require specific schooling, make the role of music among intellectuals in postwar Paris, or in almost any time and place, a thorny problem. Technical requirements also make the issue of music education, and historical developments therein, a critical matter in this study. The history of American music education beyond the primary and secondary level is a virtually untouched subject. At the libraries of various music schools in the country are some raw materials that can be put to good use. Five music schools have been the subjects of monographs. Walter Raymond Spalding, former chairman of the Harvard music department, wrote *Music at Harvard: A Historical Review of Men and Events* (New York: Coward-McCann, 1935). He also assisted Samuel Eliot Morison with a section on music at Harvard for the latter's *Three Centuries of Harvard, 1636-1936* (Cambridge: Harvard University Press, 1936). R. D. Skyrum wrote a thorough history of the Oberlin Conservatory: "Oberlin Conservatory, A Century of Musical Growth" (Ph.D. diss., University of Southern California, 1963). John Lewis wrote "An Historical Study of the Origin and Development of the Cincinnati Conservatory of Music" (D.Ed. thesis, Teachers College of the University of Cincinnati, 1943). A slightly more interesting thesis was written by Ray Edwin Robinson on the Peabody Conservatory of Baltimore: "The Peabody Conservatory: An American Solution to a European Musical Philosophy" (Ph.D. diss., Peabody Conservatory of Music, 1968). Frank Damrosch's *Institute of Musical Art, 1905-1926*, printed privately for the Juilliard School of Music, 1936, is a more informal history of the institution which merged with the Juilliard School.

Elsewhere exist assorted catalogues, memoranda, and letters which librarians at various music schools will gladly help any scholar sift through. The catalogues and memos at the Cleveland Institute of Music are most interesting, particularly for their first five years, 1920-1924, when the composer Ernst Bloch was director. The materials that he wrote, including all catalogue statements, reveal the pedagogical philosophy of a most interesting artist who has been sadly neglected by musicologists thus far. Materials at the Eastman School in Rochester, New York, are similarly revealing of Howard Hanson. A most significant theme in much of his memoranda is the view he developed regarding the important relationship of music and university education. Eastman and the University of Rochester are run by the same board and have had shifting cross-registration agreements. Hanson strongly favored close relations. At Harvard, in addition to the writings of Walter Spalding, the Nathan Pusey Library has the papers and letters of many notables of Harvard's music faculty, as well as of many other departments. Most useful to me were the materials of Spalding, John Knowles Paine, Archibald T. Davison, and Edward Burlingame Hill. The French connection discussed in Chapter 2 of this book is quite discernible here. At the New England Conservatory in Boston the chief points one can quickly detect are the dominance of a strictly musical approach, as opposed to one that emphasizes the liberal arts, the close ties to the Boston Symphony, and the stolid German orientation that went with it. Materials at the Yale School of Music reveal the degree to which Horatio Parker commanded all facets of the program in the early twentieth century. My most helpful sources there were Professors Luther Noss and Bruce Simonds, both of whom have been at Yale since the early twenties and helped give human dimension to many of the sources. Columbia University's music pedagogy in these years is best revealed, besides in the catalogs and course descriptions, in the writings of its two preeminent professors in the late nineteenth and early twentieth century— Edward MacDowell and Daniel Gregory Mason. MacDowell's lectures and other writings on music were collected and edited by W. J. Baltzell in *Critical and Historical Essays, Lectures Delivered at Columbia University by Edward MacDowell* (Boston: Arthur P. Schmidt, 1912). Mason's writings are voluminous (all published in New York by the Macmillan Company): *Contemporary Composers* (1918), *The Dilemma of American Music* (1928), *From Grieg to Brahms* (1927), *The Romantic Composers* (1936), and *Music in My Time and Other Reminiscences* (1936). As stated, New York's

Institute of Musical Art, institutional forerunner of the Juilliard School of Music; the Peabody Conservatory; and the Cincinnati Conservatory have been the subject of monographs. Catalogues and memoranda, as at other schools, provided me with occasional bits of information as well.

Regarding music education in France, the aforementioned works on French music contain some valuable materials on pedagogy. Vincent d'Indy's *Cours de Composition*, in four volumes (Paris: Durand et Fils, 1912), is a full testament to his music and esthetic philosophy. D'Indy's biography of his friend, *César Franck*, translated by Rosa Newmarch (1910; reprint ed., New York: Dover Publications, 1965), also reveals much about their shared views on pedagogy, as well as on musical issues in general. Nadia Boulanger, alas, wrote very little about music—a few articles for *Le Monde Musical* between 1918 and 1921 and *Lectures on Modern Music*, delivered under the auspices of the Rice Institute Lectureship in Music, January 27, 28, and 29, 1925, *Rice Institute Pamphlets*, vol. 13, no. 2 (April 1926). I corresponded with her a few times during the last years of her life, when she was ill and nearly blind. Her letters availed little other than a reinforcement of my perception of the humane warmth that subsumed her total dedication to the profession of teaching; I suppose I could not have asked for anything more. There is a biography of her by Alan Kendall, *The Tender Tyrant: Nadia Boulanger, A Life Devoted to Music* (London: McDonald and Jane's 1976), which contains many interesting reminiscences by people who dealt with her over the years. Most of these materials had theretofore been scattered about, so Kendall's book provides a service. Another biography, by Léonie Rosenstiel, *Nadia Boulanger: A Life in Music* (New York: W. W. Norton, 1982), has much new, valuable information, as Boulanger opened her personal papers to Rosenstiel. Unfortunately, Rosenstiel wasted her energies on furtive gossip and on such peripheral issues as Boulanger's protofeminism, or lack thereof. In 1937 Boulanger settled that issue before an energetic reporter who inquired as to her feelings about being a woman in a male-dominated profession: "I have been a woman for over fifty years, and I have gotten over my original astonishment." Copland's prediction that someday the full story of her service to music will be told has yet to come to fruition. Or perhaps it has—in the music of the thousands of composers who have passed through her salon.

Turning to the subject of the American music that emerged from Nadia Boulanger's salon, there are several important books by American composers: Virgil Thomson's autobiography and Aaron Copland's *The New Music* have already been mentioned. Elsewhere both have continued to be most articulate in their musings on the music world around them. Copland's *Music and Imagination* (Cambridge: Harvard University Press, 1952) examines the process of creating music, wherein he reveals the aesthetics and history that come forth in his mind whenever jotting notes on a score. I recommend it to any musician or listener who feels that the sweep of music history and the relationship of musical ideas to one another over time is merely a historian's intellectual construct. Copland shows just how crucial such matters are. His *Copland on Music* (1944; reprint ed., New York: W. W. Norton, 1963) is a collection of articles he wrote for different journals at various times in his career. There is no central thesis in the book. But the articles collectively indicate the composer's sensitivity to the importance of every member of the musical and artistic community: critic, composer, teacher, performer, conductor. It is this organic sense that guided his early desire to break down the unnecessary barriers between genres. His writings, musical and verbal, reveal that this sense was never lost.

Virgil Thomson is probably the most prolific and articulate writer about music of any composer in this century. His articles written as music critic for the *New York Herald Tribune* have been collected and published in *The Art of Judging Music* (New York: Alfred A. Knopf, 1948), *Music Right and Left* (New York: Greenwood Press, 1969), and *Music Reviewed* (New York: Vintage Books, 1967). He also wrote three studies of the music world around him: *American Music Since 1910* (New York: Holt, Rinehart and Winston, 1971), *The Musical Scene* (New York: Alfred A. Knopf, 1948), and *The State of Music* (New York: W. Morrow, 1939). As with the articles in the *Herald Tribune*, the subject matter here, of course, varies tremendously. But the chief issue to which Thomson, in various ways, has always been sensitive is that of artistic freedom. Stated thus it sounds a bit trite, but Thomson saw at first hand the strangulation of art with the rise of extremist politics in Europe. He also saw the more subtle, hence in some ways more dangerous, constraint of commercialism. Amidst that he stood, as critic, writer, and composer, for purity of expression against any force which would oppose that and against any composer willing to seek a short cut to success through conformity.

Roger Sessions was no less uncompromising in his idealism. His many essays on music have been collected in Edward T. Cone, ed., *Roger Sessions on Music* (Princeton: Princeton University Press, 1979). His perspective is more exclusively international than Thomson's, which often focused directly on American matters. Sessions speaks of the world of music and has the depth of philosophical expression to maintain his lofty stance. Like Thomson he opposes any facile linkage of art to politics, to nationalism, or to commercialism. Perhaps, like Solzhenitsyn, Sessions holds to ideals that modern society simply cannot attain. But it is unclear whether the resulting gap is his failure or ours.

The thoughts of Howard Hanson and Elliott Carter are seen in Howard Hanson, *Music in Contemporary American Civilization* (Lincoln: University of Nebraska Press, 1951), and Allen Edwards, *Flawed Words and Stubborn Sounds: A Conversation with Elliott Carter* (New York: W. W. Norton, 1972). Both seem much more conciliatory than Thomson, and certainly more so than Sessions. They are not more superficial, but more sensitive to the compromising nature of most artists nurtured in this century.

A most valuable volume is Henry Cowell, ed., *American Composers on American Music* (Stanford University Press, 1933). Its value, in addition to the content of each composer's article, is its bringing together the thoughts of so many worthwhile artists. The only other sources for such materials are the contemporaneous music and art journals. The most valuable of these is *Modern Music*, sometimes called the *League of Composers Review*. Published in New York from 1924 to 1946, it was the news organ for Europe and all the Americas. It regularly covered the latest trends, city by city. And it was the forum where contemporary aesthetic discussions, and battles, took place most openly. Every major composer had his or her music reviewed there, and the list of contributors is a Who's Who of twentieth-century composition and musicology. Three British journals—*Music and Letters*, *Musical Times*, and *Musical Opinion*—also focused on the modern scene,

though largely on Europe. Three other New York magazines—
Musical Quarterly, *Musical Courier*, and *Music and Man*—were,
and are, as oriented to earlier music as to the modern. Their quality
was first rate, but of less use for this study.

Secondary sources on American music abound. The best single
volume general history is Gilbert Chase's *America's Music*, second
edition (New York: McGraw-Hill Book Co., 1966). Chase covers
the music of almost every major figure in American art music and a
good deal of the vernacular tradition, with an interpretive scheme
that focuses on the transplantation of European ideas into American
soil. The older works of John Tasker Howard, *Our American
Music*, fourth edition (New York: Thomas Y. Crowell, 1965) and
Our Contemporary Composers (New York: Thomas Y. Crowell,
1941), are as comprehensive as the Chase work but straightforwardly biographical. Of similar structure, more in depth, and
strictly focusing on the American composers of the twentieth
century is Joseph Machlis, *American Composers of Our Time*
(New York: Thomas Y. Crowell Co., 1963). H. Wiley Hitchcock's
Music in the United States: A Historical Introduction (Englewood
Cliffs, N.J.: Prentice-Hall, 1969) broaches the important social
issues of (in his terms) the cultivated and the vernacular while
tracing the music of selected figures. The brevity of the work,
however, leaves one unfulfilled. This is the case with Prentice-
Hall's entire series on music. But then, the works were intended
to be introductions and nothing more. Arthur Edwards and
W. Thomas Marrocco's *Music in the United States* (Dubuque,
Iowa: William C. Brown Co., 1968) and John Rublowsky's *Music
in America* (New York: Crowell-Collier Press, 1967), like Hitchcock,
explore some interesting sociological dimensions of music in the
United States, but terribly briefly. Several good works exist that
deal with events around music: Jacques Barzun, *Music in American
Life* (1955; reprint ed., Bloomington: Indiana University Press,
1965); David Ewen, *Music Comes to America* (New York: Thomas
Y. Crowell, 1942); Irving Sablosky, *American Music* (Chicago:
University of Chicago Press, 1969); Milton Golden, *The Music
Merchants* (New York: Macmillan Co., 1969); Joseph Mussulman,
*Music in the Cultured Generations: A Social History of Music in
America, 1870-1900* (Evanston: Northwestern University Press,
1971); and John C. Mueller, *The American Symphony Orchestra:*

A Social History of Musical Taste (Bloomington: Indiana University Press, 1951). All deal with sociological and economic issues within the world of American music and on their own terms are quite useful.

Two older texts—Louis Elson, *The History of Music in America* (New York: Macmillan Co., 1904), and Frederick Louis Ritter, *Music in America* (New York: Charles Scribner's Sons, 1890)—are important as period pieces in music historiography. While their discussions of particular composers are excellent, of greater interest is what they leave out—the entire vernacular tradition. Regarding the developments in the American vernacular traditions, the two best sources on musical developments in the early twentieth century are Gunther Schuller, *The History of Jazz* (New York: Oxford University Press, 1968) and André Hodeir, *Jazz: Its Evolution and Essence*, translated by David Noakes (New York: Grove Press, 1956).

Perhaps the most interesting works on American music are by the English musicologist Wilfred Mellers: *Caliban Reborn: Renewal in Twentieth-Century Music* (New York: Harper and Row, 1967) and *Music in a New Found Land* (New York: Hillstone Publishing Co., 1975). Taking the character of Caliban from Shakespeare's *The Tempest* as a metaphor, Mellers develops the notion of America as a society where the primitive and innocent are more prevalent than in Europe. Yet, like Caliban, the primitivism and innocence of America are subject to change. Mellers thus sees the European connection as the primary force of change, and points out that this European connection is also inextricably bound to America. A dialectic thus exists, which sometimes takes the form of dialogue, sometimes of war. He sees this not as something that can or should be resolved, but rather allowed to take its course. This provides a basis for him to examine the full gamut of American music with an ever-refreshed perspective.

Within the world of American art music, some of the best sources are histories of American orchestras: M. A. DeWolf Howe, *The Boston Symphony Orchestra, 1881-1931* (Boston: Houghton Mifflin, 1931); H. Earle Johnson, *Symphony Hall, Boston* (Boston: Little, Brown and Co., 1950); Philo Adams Otis, *The Chicago Symphony Orchestra: Its Organization, Growth, and Development, 1891-1924* (Chicago: Clayton F. Summy Co., 1924); Richard

Aldrich, *Concert Life in New York, 1902-1923* (New York: G. P. Putnam's Sons, 1941); Richard Schickel, *The World of Carnegie Hall* (New York: Julian Messner, 1960); Howard Shanet, *Philharmonic: A History of New York's Orchestra* (Garden City, N.Y.: Doubleday and Co., 1975); Herbert Kupferberg, *Those Fabulous Philadelphians: The Life and Times of a Great Orchestra* (New York: Charles Scribner's Sons, 1969); and Frances Anne Wister, *Twenty-Five Years of the Philadelphia Orchestra, 1900-1925* (1925; reprint ed., Freeport, N.Y.: Books for Libraries Press, 1971). The impoverished exclusivity of such musical organizations, like the problems inherent in the separation of the vernacular and art music worlds discussed in this book, is revealed quite clearly in Edward Arian, *Bach, Beethoven, and Bureaucracy: The Case of the Philadelphia Orchestra* (Montgomery: University of Alabama Press, 1971), the title of which is self-explanatory.

Several local studies of music in the United States are quite good. These authors examine all levels of musical activity without elitism in either direction, allowing, be it history or music, for only two kinds of art, good and bad: Bruce Bastin, *Crying for the Carolinas* (London: November Books, 1971); George Thornton Edwards, *Music and the Musicians of Maine* (Portland, Maine: Southworth Press, 1928); F. Karl Grossman, *A History of Music in Cleveland* (Cleveland: Case Western Reserve University Press, 1972); Frances Hall Johnson, *Musical Memories of Hartford* (New York: AMS Press, 1970); Lubov Keefer, *Baltimore's Music: The Haven of the American Composer* (Baltimore: J. H. Furst Co., 1962); Ernst C. Krohn, *A Century of Missouri Music* (St. Louis: Private Printing, 1924); Lota M. Spell, *Music in Texas* (New York: American Musicological Society, 1973); Howard Swan, *Music in the Southwest, 1825-1950* (San Marino, Calif.: Huntington Library, 1952); and Malcolm G. Wyer and Edwin J. Stringham, *Music in Denver and Colorado* (Denver: Denver Public Library, 1927).

As my narrative, and at times my tone, have indicated, there was a split in American music between the art and vernacular music worlds. My attempt to tell the story of trends in the distinct art music sphere led me to examine the values of those who seemed to favor such a split—music critics. Accordingly, I perused numerous newpapers of the late nineteenth and early twentieth century: for New York City, the *Evening Post, Herald, Journal, Sun, Times, Tribune,* and *World;* for Boston, the *Christian Science Monitor* and *Evening Times;* for Philadelphia, the *Public Ledger* and *Tribune;* and for Chicago, the *Defender, Herald, Herald Examiner, Daily Inter-Ocean, Record Herald,* and *Tribune.* Some of the major music critics also wrote monographs, further revealing of their sensibilities: John Sullivan Dwight, *Journal of Music (1852-1881)* (New York: Johnson Reprint, 1967); Henry T. Finck: *My Adventures in the Golden Age of Music* (New York: Funk and Wagnalls, 1926), *Success in Music and How It Is Won* (New York: Scribner's, 1909), and *Wagner and His Works* (New York: Scribner's, 1896); Louis Elson: *European Reminiscences, Musical and Otherwise* (Chicago: Manual Publishing Co., 1891), *Famous Composers and Their Works* (Boston: J. B. Millet Co., 1900), *Great Composers and Their Work* (Boston: L. C. Page and Co., 1910), *The National Music of America and Its Sources* (Boston: L. C. Page and Co., 1911), *The Realm of Music* (Boston: New England Conservatory, 1892), and *Women in Music* (1918; reprint ed., New York: Gordon Press, 1976); James Gibbons Huneker: *Mezzotints in Modern Music* (New York: Scribner's, 1899), *Old Fogy, His Musical Opinions and Grotesques* (Philadelphia: T. Presser Co., 1913), and *Overtones, A Book of Temperaments: Strauss, Parsifal, Verdi, Balzac, Flaubert, Nietzsche, and Turgenieff* (New York: Scribner's, 1904). A bit less antivernacular was Lawrence Gilman, and much less so was Paul Rosenfeld. Gilman's views can be found in *Aspects of Modern Opera* (1909; reprint ed., New York: Haskell House Publishers, 1969), *The Music of Tomorrow and Other Studies* (New York: John Lane Co., 1907), *Nature in Music and Other Studies in the Tone Poetry of Today* (New York: John Lane Co., 1914), and *Phases of Modern Music* (New York: Harper and Brothers, 1904); Rosenfeld's views can be found in *Discoveries of a Music Critic* (New York: Harcourt, Brace and Co., 1936), *An Hour with American Music* (Philadelphia: J. B. Lippincott, 1929), Herbert Leibowitz, ed., *Musical Impressions: Selections of Paul Rosenfeld's Criticism* (New York: Hill and Wang, 1969), and *Musical Portraits: Interpretations of Twenty Modern Composers* (New York: Harcourt, Brace and Co., 1920). Of great enjoyment, though more from a literary than a musical standpoint, are the articles on music by H. L. Mencken in Louis Cheslock, ed., *H. L. Mencken on Music* (New York: Schirmer Books, 1975).

Musical scores have been the most primary "documents" in the preparation of this book. The following were the most important:

George Antheil, *Ballet Mécanique* (New York: Templeton Publishing Co., 1954).

   Piano Sonata no. 2, "The Airplane" (New York: New Music Edition, 1931).

Marion Bauer, Four Piano Pieces (New York: Cos Cob, 1930).

   I Love the Night (New York: Schirmer, 1924).

   In the Bosom of the Desert (New York: Schirmer, 1924).

   Midsummer Dreams (New York: Schirmer, 1924).

Dudley Buck, *The Golden Legend* (New York: Schirmer, 1880).

   Light of Asia (New York: Schirmer, 1884).

John Alden Carpenter, *Adventures in a Perambulator* (New York: Schirmer, 1920).

   Concertino for Piano and Orchestra (New York: Schirmer, 1920).

George Chadwick, Overture to *Rip Van Winkle* (Boston: A. P. Schmidt, 1879).

   Overture to *Thalia* (Boston: A. P. Schmidt, 1883).

   Symphonic Ballad, *Tam O'Shanter* (Boston: A. P. Schmidt, 1911).

   Symphonic Sketches (Boston: A. P. Schmidt, 1907).

Aaron Copland, *Appalachian Spring* (New York: Boosey and Hawkes, 1944).

   As It Fell Upon a Day (New York: Boosey and Hawkes, 1929).

   Billy the Kid (New York: Boosey and Hawkes, 1941).

   The Cat and the Mouse (New York: Boosey and Hawkes, 1950).

   Concerto for Piano and Orchestra (New York: Boosey and Hawkes, 1956).

   Dance Symphony (New York: Arrow Music Press, 1931).

   Fanfare for the Common Man (New York: Boosey and Hawkes, 1944).

   Grogh (New York: Cos Cob, 1925).

   Hear Ye! Hear Ye! (New York: Cos Cob, 1934).

   Lincoln Portrait (New York: Boosey and Hawkes, 1942).

   Music for the Theatre (New York: Boosey and Hawkes, 1960).

   Passacaglia (New York: Cos Cob, 1922).

   Piano Variations (New York: Boosey and Hawkes, 1959).

   Rodeo (New York: Boosey and Hawkes, 1942).

Symphonic Ode (New York: Cos Cob, 1930).
Symphony for Organ and Orchestra (New York: Boosey and Hawkes, 1963).
Two Pieces for String Quartet (New York: Cos Cob, 1928).
Vitebsk (New York: Cos Cob, 1929).
Claude Debussy, *The Children's Corner* (Paris: Durand, 1910).
Preludes for Piano (Paris: Durand, 1910).
Antonín Dvořák, Quartet in F (Berlin: Eulenburg, n.d.).
Quintet (Prague: Statni, 1955).
Symphony in E. Minor *(From the New World)* (New York: Kalmus, 1932).
G. Herbert Elwell, Piano Sonata (New York: Oxford University Press, 1926).
George Gershwin, *An American in Paris* (New York: New World Music Corp., 1930).
Concerto in F (New York: Harms Inc., 1927).
Rhapsody in Blue (New York: Harms Inc., 1927).
Louis Moreau Gottschalk, *The Banjo* (New York: Schirmer, 1962).
La Nuit des Tropiques (New York: Theodore Presser, 1956).
Pasquinade (photocopy of original score, University of Wisconsin Music Library).
Piano Works (New York: Dover, 1973).
Charles Thomlinson Griffes, *Four Roman Sketches* (New York: Schirmer, 1917).
The Pleasure Dome of Kubla Khan (New York: Schirmer, 1922).
Poem for Flute and Orchestra (New York: Schirmer, 1951).
Howard Hanson, *The Lament of Beowolf* (New York: C. C. Buchard and Co., 1925).
Nordic Symphony (New York: C. C. Buchard and Co., 1922).
North and West (New York: C. C. Buchard and Co., 1923).
Symphonic Legend (New York: C. C. Buchard and Co., 1920).
Roy Harris, *American Portraits* (New York: Cos Cob, 1929).
Concerto for Clarinet, Piano, and String Quartet (New York: Cos Cob, 1927).
Impressions on a Rainy Day (New York: Cos Cob, 1926).
Piano Sonata (New York: Cos Cob, 1928).
String Quartet (New York: Cos Cob, 1929).
Symphony no. 3 (New York: Schirmer, 1940).
Toccata for Orchestra (New York: Carl Fischer, 1950).
When Johnny Comes Marching Home (New York: Schirmer, 1935).
Arthur Honegger, *Le Roi David* (New York: Schirmer, 1924).
Concertino for Piano and Orchestra (Paris: Editions Salabert, 1926).
Ernst Křenek, *Jonny Spielt Auf* (New York: J. Boonin, 1954).

Charles Loeffler, *Memories of My Childhood in a Russian Village* (New York: Schirmer, 1925).

La Mort de Tintagiles (New York: Schirmer, 1906).

A Pagan Poem (New York: Schirmer, 1909).

Edward MacDowell, Concerto for Piano and Orchestra in A Minor (Berlin: Breitkopf, 1910).

Hamlet and Ophelia (Boston: Schmidt, 1885).

Launcelot and Elaine (Boston: Schmidt, 1888).

New England Idyls (New York: Schirmer, n.d.).

Orchestral Suite no. 1 (Boston: Schmidt, 1891).

Orchestral Suite no. 2 (Boston: Schmidt, 1897).

Woodland Sketches (Boston: Schmidt, 1896).

Daniel Gregory Mason, *Country Pictures* (New York: Schirmer, 1913).

Passacaglia and Fugue (New York: Schirmer, 1914).

Quartet on Negro Themes (New York: Schirmer, 1930).

Darius Milhaud, *Le Boeuf sur la Toit* (Paris: La Sirène Musicale, 1920).

La Création du Monde (Paris: Max Esching, 1920).

Saudades do Brazil (Paris: Esching, 1922).

Douglas Moore, *Moby Dick* (New York: Carl Fischer, 1928).

The Pageant of P. T. Barnum (New York: Carl Fischer, 1924).

A Symphony of Autumn (New York: Carl Fischer, 1930).

John Knowles Paine, Mass in D (Boston: Schmidt, 1868).

Symphony in A (Boston: Schmidt, 1880).

Symphony in C Minor (New York: DeCapo Press, 1972).

Horatio Parker, *Hora Novissima* (New York: DeCapo Press, 1972).

Fairyland (New York: Schirmer, 1915).

Mona (New York: Schirmer, 1911).

Walter Piston, Sonata for Flute and Piano (New York: Associated Music Publishers, 1933).

Suite for Oboe and Piano (New York: Schirmer, 1974).

Suite for Orchestra (New York: Cos Cob, 1929).

Quincy Porter, Sonata no. 1 for Violin, Flute, and Piano (New York: Schirmer, 1933).

Sonata no. 2 for Violin and Piano (New York: Schirmer, 1933).

String Quartet in E Minor (New York: Schirmer, 1935).

String Quartet in G Minor (New York: Schirmer, 1935).

Maurice Ravel, *L'Enfant at les Sortilèges* (Paris: Durand, 1925).

Piano Concerto (Philadelphia: Elkan-Vocal, 1932).

Violin Sonata (Paris: Durand, 1927).

Erik Satie, *Parade* (Paris: Rouart, Lerolle, 1917).

Rogert Sessions, Concerto for Violin and Orchestra (New York: Edgar Stillman Kelly Society, 1937).

On the Beach at Fontana, words by James Joyce (London: British
Continental Music Agencies, 1964).
Suite from *The Black Maskers* (New York: Cos Cob, 1928).
Igor Stravinsky, *L'Histoire d'un Soldat* (London: J. W. Chester, 1924).
Ragtime for Eleven Instruments (London: J. W. Chester, 1920).
Virgil Thomson, *Capital, Capitals* (New York: Boosey and Hawkes, 1968).
Five Songs from William Blake (New York: G. Ricordi, 1953).
Four Saints in Three Acts (New York: Arrow Music Press, 1948).
String Quartets nos. 1 and 2 (New York: Boosey and Hawkes, 1958).
Symphony on a Hymn Tune (New York: Southern Music Publish-
ing Co., 1954).

INDEX

About the Author

Alan Howard Levy is Assistant Professor of History at the University of Louisville in Kentucky. His articles on American musical history have appeared in *Contemporary French Civilization* and the *Bulletin of the Council for Research in Music Education.*

DATE DUE

GAYLORD   PRINTED IN U.S.A.